✵

KHRUSHCHEV: THE YEARS IN POWER

NIKITA S. KHRUSHCHEV IN 1959

KHRUSHCHEV

THE YEARS IN POWER

roy a. medvedev

zhores a. medvedev

OXFORD UNIVERSITY PRESS · 1977

LONDON OXFORD MELBOURNE

Translated by Andrew R. Durkin

Oxford University Press, Walton Street, Oxford OX2 6DP

OXFORD LONDON GLASGOW NEW YORK
TORONTO MELBOURNE WELLINGTON CAPE TOWN
IBADAN NAIROBI DAR ES SALAAM LUSAKA ADDIS ABABA
KUALA LUMPUR SINGAPORE JAKARTA HONG KONG TOKYO
DELHI BOMBAY CALCUTTA MADRAS KARACHI

ISBN 0 19 215835 X

Copyright © 1975 (Russian edition), 1976
(English-language edition) Columbia University Press

First published in English by Columbia University
Press, 1976. This edition first published 1977.

Printed in Great Britain by offset lithography by
Billing & Sons Limited,
Guildford, London and Worcester.

contents

preface

THIS book, despite its modest length, is the result of an extended though intermittent effort begun in 1963. It was then that Khrushchev's headstrong and ill-planned agricultural ventures brought on a grave economic crisis and forced the Soviet Union to purchase grain from outside its borders for the first time in its history or, indeed, in the entire history of Russia.*

My own interest in Khrushchev's political and economic reforms arose in connection with my research on the history of a controversy in Soviet genetics, the subject of my book *The Rise and Fall of T. D. Lysenko.†* For my brother and co-author Roy, an analysis of Khrushchev's policies developed naturally from his work on the history of Stalinism, published as *Let History Judge.‡* Roy and I also had published several articles on Khrushchev's agricultural policy in the *samizdat* (underground) journal *Politichesky dnevnik* (Political Diary), which circulated in Moscow from 1964 to 1971.

Our study of Khrushchev was temporarily and rudely interrupted in 1971. When, in October of that year, it became known that *Let History Judge* was soon to appear in the United States, the KGB (Committee of State Security) searched Roy's apart-

---

* "Russia," of course, refers to our country as it was before 1917; the "Soviet Union" to it as it was organized after the Russian Revolution.

† Zhores A. Medvedev, *The Rise and Fall of T. D. Lysenko*, trans. by I. M. Lerner (New York: Columbia University Press, 1969).

‡ Roy A. Medvedev, *Let History Judge*, trans. by C. Taylor (New York: Knopf, 1971).

ment and all of his research materials on Stalin were confiscated, as were all his notes and materials on Khrushchev (even including clippings from Soviet newspapers). Nevertheless, in 1972 we were able to begin our work over again, using our articles in *Political Diary* as a basis. The present version of this book was completed in 1974, the political chapters being written by me in London.

I have assumed all responsibility for the publication of the entire book. I emphasize this point simply because Roy, who is subject to Soviet law, is more restricted in his actions and lacks the freedom of contact with Western publishers available to me as one who resides outside the Soviet Union (an enforced exile caused by my having been deprived of my passport and my Soviet citizenship). Because of censorship entanglements, the impossibility of sending manuscripts to the Soviet Union has prevented me from showing the final text of the book, and particularly the changes suggested by pre-publication reviewers, to Roy for his approval.

In the West, quite an extensive literature on Khrushchev exists, and several biographies have been written. In the Soviet Union, not only are there no books on Khrushchev, but since 1964 his name has not even been mentioned in the Soviet press except for a brief item announcing his death in 1971. There are no monographs on Khrushchev even in *samizdat,* nor are there any memoirs devoted to him. The Stalin era has received incomparably more attention in *samizdat* writing than has the Khrushchev period. When Roy and I were working on our respective books on Stalin and Lysenko, we had at our disposal dozens of memoirs, critical essays, and a wealth of unpublished documents and other materials, but nothing comparable on Khrushchev appeared after his removal from power in 1964. This book is in fact the first by Russian authors on Khrushchev and the first to attempt to analyze his reforms and his policies from the viewpoint of people who perceived those reforms "from within."

Khrushchev's own memoirs, published in two volumes in the West, 1971 and 1974, did not have any great value as a source for our work. In his memoirs, Khrushchev mainly discusses international problems and treats his own biography and political career without documentation and with no self-critical analysis of the many political and economic errors he made. He also avoids discussion of his agricultural policy, an analysis of which forms the central theme of our book.

The numerous works on Khrushchev written in the West contain interesting and extensive factual material, but still they are analyses "from outside," academic dissections of events in another country whose internal mechanisms have not always been fully understood by the authors of these books.

For Roy and for me, Khrushchev and his times are a still living history—we participated in the hopes and disenchantments of the period; we experienced enthusiasm and bitterness, elation at his bold political and diplomatic reforms, and exasperation at his sometimes startling ignorance when it came to handling simple economic, agronomic, and theoretical problems. It is painful to contemplate how much Khrushchev, after a brilliant start, could have done for the Soviet Union and the whole world, yet his contribution turned out to be extremely limited by the time he reached the end of his political career with an abruptness inevitable in the crisis situation that developed in 1963 and 1964. In this book, we want to record the atmosphere of the Khrushchev period as it was felt by those living within the Soviet Union.

For this reason we do not intend to present a comprehensive biography of Nikita Khrushchev, nor a complete history of the Khrushchev years. Much of what happened in this comparatively recent time has been discussed in a number of books of various sorts. A major contributor has been Khrushchev himself, for besides his memoirs, Khrushchev had published numerous volumes of his own speeches on international questions, agricultural problems, and other concerns—including statements about the "responsibilities" of literature and the arts. All these volumes, as well as most of the diplomatic shifts taken at his direction, provide a striking demonstration of his constant activity, of his genuine achievements in reducing international tensions, and of his supreme control over all aspects of life in the Soviet Union. It is not our intention to recapitulate, even in a condensed form, everything that was done by Khrushchev or that took place while he was in power.

It is not difficult to explain Khrushchev's rise to the heights occupied by Lenin and Stalin (the power to *personally* direct all foreign and domestic policy, alter Party programs and rules, appoint or dismiss political aspirants, propose and push through new laws)—his rise does not challenge the historian's ability to explain or assess. However Khrushchev's fall poses a much greater challenge; unexpected by the rest of the world, it caused great astonishment. In the Soviet Union, it had been considered to be only a matter of time and therefore was accepted without undue excitement. Khrushchev's metamorphosis from the cautious and methodical reformer of 1953–57 (it should be remembered that he was at that time still under the restraining influence of an entrenched and conservative opposition) to an impetuous iconoclast after he attained full power is a fascinating subject for study. Khrushchev of course did accomplish much that was positive after 1957, and perhaps would have done still more after 1964 if he had remained in charge. But it must be acknowledged that, from 1958 on, he was leading the nation to the brink of economic catastrophe and the unfortunate aftereffects of many of the projects and programs of 1958–64 are still being felt in the Soviet Union at present.

In the most active period of *samizdat* (1962–66), Soviet authors were able to let initial versions of their critical writings circulate freely among knowledgeable fellow Soviet citizens, a practice which brought much fresh and original material, as well as helpful criticism, to these works. Such favorable circumstances for "internal" circulation of manuscripts no longer exist. Therefore we, the authors, hope that this book will aid in the gathering of new, unique, and previously unknown material on Khrushchev's domestic policies and will in the future serve as a basis for further analyses of the problems we have raised.

ZHORES A. MEDVEDEV

London
January 1976

THE SOVIET UNION — EVENTS AND

TRADITIONAL AGRICULTURAL REGIONS

- Black earth zone (but prone to summer drought)
- Central zone (adequate rainfall but poor soil)
- Chiefly rye-growing regions
- Cotton, corn, vineyards
- Upper limit of corn belt before 1954

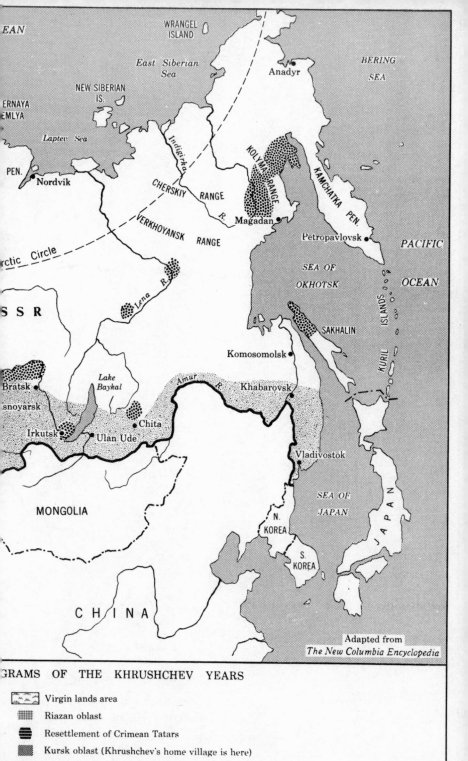

Adapted from
The New Columbia Encyclopedia

GRAMS OF THE KHRUSHCHEV YEARS

Virgin lands area

Riazan oblast

Resettlement of Crimean Tatars

Kursk oblast (Khrushchev's home village is here)

Pitsunda promontory, site of Khrushchev's summer villa

Prison / slave labor camps

chapter one

THE
STALIN INHERITANCE

O<small>UR</small> plan in this book is first to set the stage for
the drama of Khrushchev and his decade of
power by describing the immediate background—Stalin's legacy
of terror, the subdued but unrelenting power struggle after his
death, and Khrushchev's early tentative attempts at agricultural
and political reform, reforms that were sensitively tuned to the
needs and desires of ordinary citizens. We will then turn to our
main theme—those disruptive economic policies and political
shocks that Khrushchev so mercilessly heaped on a bewildered
people. If "too little, too late" can be catastrophic in war, too
much, too soon can be equally disastrous for a nation.

Our "list" of the reasons for Khrushchev's fall is not a mere
repetition of those rumored but as yet unpublished accusations
against Khrushchev that were put forth in a "confidential" explanation circulated among Party enclaves after October 1964.
In large measure, our analysis is independent and points out
flaws not only in Khrushchev's own character, but also in the
whole pyramid of power of that time, defects of the social sys-

tem carried over from Stalin and only slightly altered under Khrushchev.

TOO MANY HEIRS

The death of Joseph Stalin in March 1953 created a unique political vacuum. In the final years of his life, Stalin had trusted no one, not even his closest associates. Because of his continual fear of being overthrown, he did not leave a political bequest of any sort or name a political successor. (In 1923, Lenin, sensing the approach of death, had written a testament in the form of a letter to the Party Congress, giving in it his own evaluations of the other leaders who surrounded him. Ironically his principal recommendation—that Stalin be shifted away from the center of power—was not carried out.) Stalin gave little thought to the time when he would die, and even on the eve of his death was planning a new, radical purge of prominent political figures. The old Politburo, a small elite group who headed the Party's Central Committee, had been reorganized into a broader Presidium composed of some thirty members, but not one of them could (or would) have said that he was Stalin's heir.

Real power rested, even though temporarily, in the hands of Georgy Malenkov (a deputy premier) and Lavrenti Beria (chief of state security), with whom Vyacheslav Molotov (one-time foreign minister) allied himself as well. After World War II, Stalin had exercised his dictatorial power through government channels rather than through Party apparatus, primarily as Chairman of the Council of Ministers (i.e., Premier) of the Soviet Union. The role of the Party's Central Committee was reduced and the position of its General Secretary converted to First Secretary *—the position from which Stalin once had wielded absolute power over the country. He now found it more

---

* "First Secretary" designated the chairman of the Party Secretariat. "General Secretary" meant the leader of the whole Party.

convenient to exercise dictatorial power directly, as head (or chairman) of the Soviet government and head of the *executive* power, rather than indirectly, as Party leader. The head-of-government post was also a more convenient one for controlling the entire postwar empire he had created and for taking international action in the name of the Soviet government. Thus the key position after Stalin's death was that of Premier.*

Beria could not immediately lay claim to the premiership because, in the final months of Stalin's life, he had been deprived of some of his power in that he no longer had sole command of the repressive machinery of the MGB. The indirect cause was Stalin's final terror maneuver, the so-called "Doctors' Plot." †
Among those arrested was a protégé of Beria's, V. Abakumov, then head of the MGB. He was replaced by S. Ignatiev, a protégé of Malenkov's. Ignatiev, newly arrived from the staff of the Central Committee, had not yet had time to purge Beria's numerous supporters before Stalin died.

The day after the announcement of Stalin's death, a joint meeting of the Central Committee, the Council of Ministers, and the Presidium of the Supreme Soviet of the USSR was held to decide who would run the country. At Beria's suggestion, Malenkov was designated Premier. Accepting this post, Malenkov repaid the favor by proposing a merger of the ministries of Internal Affairs (MVD) and State Security (MGB) into one and the appointment of Lavrenti Beria as its head. Molotov became

---

* Stalin controlled the Party apparatus through Malenkov, who was accorded the signal honor of presenting the Report of the Central Committee at the Nineteenth Party Congress in 1952, the first person other than Stalin to do so since 1923.

† A number of doctors, most of them Jewish, were charged with being Zionists and/or agents of foreign intelligence organizations. They were accused of deliberately mishandling the medical treatment of highly placed public officials—of prolonging their illnesses or even bringing about their deaths. This became known as the Doctors' Plot, but the whole scheme was only an invention of Stalin's and the charges groundless, as those who abetted the persecutions well knew.

the First Deputy Premier and regained control of the Ministry of Foreign Affairs (lost to him earlier when he had incurred Stalin's displeasure). K. E. Voroshilov, also out of favor with Stalin, became Chairman of the Presidium of the Supreme Soviet. At the same time, the Presidium of the Central Committee was reduced from thirty members to only ten, listed in the following order: Malenkov, Beria, Molotov, Voroshilov, Khrushchev, Bulganin, Kaganovich, Mikoyan, Saburov, and Pervukhin. The sequence was important because it indicated, as was customary, rank in the power structure. At the time Khrushchev, then, was only No. 5.

The question of who was to head the Central Committee was not settled at this meeting, but an earlier announcement had declared that since it was essential for Khrushchev to concentrate on his work in the Secretariat of the Central Committee, he would be relieved of his duties as Secretary of the Moscow Party organization. Although Khrushchev was in charge of staging the spectacle of Stalin's funeral, it was Malenkov, Molotov, and Beria who delivered the orations. Within the Soviet Union and abroad, these three men were believed to be the ruling triumvirate.

As early as March 14, 1953, the Central Committee accepted Malenkov's resignation from the position of Secretary of the Party's Central Committee so that he could devote himself to his role as Premier. Khrushchev was chosen to take over the Party post. For reasons unknown, this resolution was not published until March 22.

Khrushchev's new appointment roused no suspicion that a successor to Stalin was emerging. No one, either within the Party or in the country at large, had the foresight to regard Khrushchev as a major figure in Soviet leadership. Besides Khrushchev, the Secretariat of the Central Committee was composed of M. A. Suslov, P. N. Pospelov, N. N. Shatalin, and S. D. Ignatiev. Only Khrushchev was also a member of the Presidium. The Secretariat had a decidedly intra-party function. It could not give directives to the Supreme Soviet; Khrushchev had no authority over Malenkov, who was the one person known best nationally in the first weeks after Stalin's death. Almost all of Khrushchev's colleagues considered him to be hardworking but uninspired, therefore hardly a political figure of national stature. They believed he was weak in political theory, a rather ordinary, sometimes crude man who would never aspire to excessive power and who would always pay dutiful attention to the opinions of "his betters"—the more experienced Party leaders.

Out of fear of one another, Stalin's associates made the same mistake that those around the ailing Lenin had made thirty years before. Then, it had been Kamenev and Zinoviev who had energetically supported Stalin for General Secretary of the Central Committee on the assumption that this little-known Georgian would not crave power. Lenin was still the actual leader of the Party and the members of Lenin's Politburo tried to keep the more prestigious posts in their own hands. However, the death of Lenin, followed shortly by the deaths of Dzherzhinsky (secret police) and Frunze (armed forces), quickly changed the distribution of power in the governing nucleus and the position of General Secretary acquired key importance.

Although in 1953 Malenkov, as head of the Soviet government, had the broadest overall influence, in local hierarchies at regional and republic levels Party secretaries remained highly powerful, and this entire Party network was now more closely linked to Khrushchev than to Malenkov. As head of government, Stalin had made all decisions directly, ignoring the Party apparatus. As Malenkov did not yet enjoy comparable authority, the relative significance of the Central Committee as the real standard-bearer of the "dictatorship of the working class" soared after the death of Stalin.

One reason why Khrushchev got the post of First Secretary

was that he had the reputation of being an expert in agricultural matters, and agriculture was the sector of the economy that was worst off and most in need of attention in 1953. Thus the advancement of Khrushchev had symbolic significance—it alleviated feelings of dissatisfaction and even despair that had been growing in the villages for many years. Khrushchev's presence among the Party's leaders gave villagers, almost crushed between terror and hunger, some hope of a change for the better.

The underestimation of the strength of the Secretariat was to cost Malenkov, Molotov, Beria, and Kaganovich dearly. In a one-party state, only a Party Congress, or a general meeting or plenum of the Central Committee in the intervals between Congresses, exercises effective power. But during the last fifteen years of Stalin's life only one Party Congress had been called, and the Party plenums had been called a few times only. Even the august group at the top of the Party pyramid, the full Politburo, which considered only the most vital issues, almost never met. Stalin usually made all major decisions either solo or after consultation with one or two of his closest associates. Only afterward were they announced as coming from the Central Committee or the Council of Ministers.

Unlike Stalin, Khrushchev, as First Secretary, did not have sufficient power to resolve even intra-party issues on his own, let alone governmental or international problems. Thus he had no choice but to convene plenums and meetings of the Presidium of the Central Committee in order to draw on the authority of these bodies. The tradition of periodic Central Committee plenums had to be revived to provide a tribune for the escalating prestige and influence of a new Party leader.

Although the principle of "collective leadership" was proclaimed after Stalin's death, the age-old tradition of the Russian nation and the thirty-five-year-old tradition of the Soviet Union demanded the rise to preeminence of a single supreme leader, firmly managing the country's affairs. After the first weeks of "collective leadership," it became obvious to an astute observer that only Malenkov, Molotov, or Khrushchev had all the attributes of such a leader. Voroshilov and Kaganovich quickly faded into the background. Voroshilov was too old and his responsibility for many defeats at the beginning of the German invasion had not been forgotten. Kaganovich was a Jew, and the anti-semitism that had been fanned by Stalin in the last years of his regime had not yet been extinguished. Beria headed an organization which, though it was extremely powerful, did not provide a stage for the public appearances, speeches, and economic and political decisions necessary to create the popular image of a leader.

THE ELIMINATION OF BERIA

In the first volume of Khrushchev's memoirs,* some aspects of Beria's "conspiracy" and Khrushchev's "counter-conspiracy" are described, along with the circumstances of Beria's arrest and subsequent execution. Unfortunately, in these reminiscences, Khrushchev gives a contradictory and imprecise account of these events and does not explain the actual nature of Beria's "conspiracy" in a concrete or reliable way. But other sources tell us little more about the crushing of Beria's own enclave within the state security organization which undoubtedly did exist and which in all probability was preparing for a seizure of power. While each of the leaders kept a wary eye on the others, Beria was the one most feared and mistrusted by all. This can be easily understood when one considers the nature and modus operandi of the MVD organization.

Behind the scenes, but foremost in the mind of any politically ambitious individual, was the state security organization, or secret police. Whatever it was called—GPU, NKVD, or MGB—this

* *Khrushchev Remembers* (New York: Little, Brown, 1971).

apparatus of terror, independent of Party control, embraced all the functions of legal and judicial procedure—arrest, investigation, trial, and imposition and execution of sentence. Stalin had made this system subordinate to himself alone. An NKVD/MGB chief of a raion (district) or oblast (region) could arrest any Party leader, even the First Secretary of the raion or oblast, or even the entire oblast/raion committee—such arrests did occur during the years of terror. The raion security organization controlled a network of secret agents ("informers") who were sometimes paid but who were more often unpaid individuals threatened into "volunteering."

Although in theory the country was controlled by the Party, this powerful system of state security, subordinate only to Stalin, loomed over all. Any Party or government figure could disappear without a trace and no mention of the arrest, trial, or execution would appear in the press, particularly if the victim had been generally liked.

In 1949, the secret police apparatus was autonomous to the extent that within departments of the Party Central Committee itself, there were "special sections" responsible not to the Central Committee, but to the MGB. The MGB had the right to inspect the desks, files, and safes of Central Committee members. Guards stationed at Central Committee office buildings were answerable to the MGB. On the other hand, Stalin, never fully trusting Beria, established an autonomous personal guard composed of troops wearing MGB uniforms but not under the control of the Minister of State Security. They were directly subordinate to Stalin and had the power, if he so ordered, to arrest any government figure, even Beria and his staff. This guard, normally stationed around Stalin's residences in the Kremlin, outside Moscow, in the Crimea, near Sochi, etc., was under the command of Nikolai Vlasik, a Soviet Army general, and not a member of the MGB forces. General Vlasik was personally dedicated to Stalin and had devotedly served as his chief bodyguard for more than twenty years. However, in 1952, Stalin, driven by his persecution mania, ordered the arrest even of General Vlasik.

After Stalin's death Beria drew this all encompassing control into his own hands, reorganized it to further his own ambitions, and appointed men committed only to himself. His empire extended into the security agencies of most of the countries of Eastern Europe. He had backed Malenkov for Premier because they had been friends of long standing—and jointly responsible for a number of wide-scale repressions.

At the time of Stalin's grandiose funeral, hundreds of thousands of people from all parts of the Soviet Union converged on Moscow. Beria ordered several divisions of MVD forces to the city to maintain order. Part of these forces were stationed in the center of the city in various administrative buildings. After the funeral, these divisions were not sent back to their regular posts. Some explanation had to be given and Beria saw to it that one was available.

Shortly after Stalin's death a general amnesty had been declared for all prisoners serving sentences of less than five years. Political prisoners (whose minimum term was normally eight years and could be as high as twenty-five) did not benefit from this amnesty, nor did dangerous common criminals or recidivists. However, contrary to the provisions of the amnesty proclamation, Beria ordered that several prison camps simply be closed down, thus releasing thousands of common criminals and recidivists, regardless of length of sentence. When they appeared in Moscow and other cities, crime rates soared along with public indignation. Thus Beria had his explanation: the preservation of order demanded the retention of large contingents of MVD forces in the cities, troops answerable to him.

Beria had good reason to accelerate his drive for power. The general amnesty for petty criminals and the release of a few carefully selected political prisoners (see chapter 2) gave a glimmer of hope and resulted in a growing popular pressure for further releases. The MVD, the Party Central Committee, and the Presidium of the Supreme Soviet were flooded with requests from people demanding the return of their loved ones. Any probe by the Central Committee into the situation and its ramifications would have been fatal for Beria. Hence his wish to keep his MVD forces in Moscow long after Stalin's funeral.

However, a conspiracy against Beria was already being organized in the Central Committee. Khrushchev and many other leaders understood the danger of total power in Beria's hands, and even Malenkov felt compelled to join them. At the head of the conspiracy stood Khrushchev, supported by the military establishment, most importantly by Marshal G. K. Zhukov.

On the day of Beria's arrest at the end of June,* his MVD guard at the Kremlin and the Central Committee buildings was replaced by regular troops and many top-rank MVD supporters of Beria were arrested. Army units, under the command of Marshals Zhukov and Konev, surrounded and blockaded the central MVD buildings in Moscow. Over several days most regional MVD officials were arrested, as were MVD ministers in the republics. Also arrested were Beria's friends V. N. Merkulov (State Control) and M. D. Bagirov (First Secretary of Azerbaidzhan and a candidate member of the Presidium).†

Investigators in the Beria case wanted witnesses for every step of his career and above all for the time when he was Secre-

---

* The arrest was made on June 28, but not reported in the press until July 10.

† According to several eyewitness accounts, practically all the officials of the central MVD administration on Dzerzhinsky Square were arrested right in their offices. Several of the most prominent and purportedly dangerous of Beria's aides were shot on the spot and their bodies transported out of town and buried.

tary of the Central Committee of the Transcaucasus and Georgia. But virtually none of these witnesses were left to tell the tale for, after he became head of the NKVD, Beria methodically annihilated almost all of his Russian co-workers in the Transcaucasus. It was necessary to search through the camps. Only two witnesses were found alive: A. V. Snegov, who had worked with Beria in the Transcaucasus, and O. G. Shatunovskaya, who had known him in Azerbaidzhan. They were flown to Moscow to give evidence, although they were still under sentence. (Snegov did not even have time to change his prison garb before arriving in Moscow.) After the trial, Snegov was reinstated, made a lieutenant-colonel in the KGB, and given an important post in the Gulag system of prison camps. He then began to compile documentation of Stalin's crimes and report directly to Khrushchev.*

The full text of Beria's indictment was read only at closed meetings of the Party elite and was much more detailed and wide-ranging than the Final Indictment (as it was called) that eventually appeared in the newspapers. It revealed the existence of an unsuspected monster—an accumulation of information about repression and terror on a scale that even Khrushchev and other prominent Party workers could scarcely comprehend. As we have seen, the MVD and the Gulag system of camps had been kept quite distant from the Party system; indeed, Party figures had no desire whatever to interfere in—or even think about—the operation of the Gulag empire. But once the decision was made to investigate Beria and his methods, many details about the flouting of judicial procedure and other

* After Khrushchev's dismissal, Snegov was retired on pension but continued, now as an historian, to amass documentation against Stalin and give a number of lectures. In 1967, when a seventy-year-old pensioner, he was accused of anti-Party activity and was once again expelled from the Party. Snegov provided many interesting documents annotating events for the history of Stalinism written by Roy A. Medvedev, *Let History Judge* (New York: Knopf, 1971).

civil rights by the NKVD/MGB apparatus inevitably became known to Party leaders and to Khrushchev.

For Beria the events of 1953 moved with unwelcome rapidity. Stalin had died in early March; by the end of June, Beria was under arrest; before the end of the year he had been tried and executed.

chapter two

VICTIMS
OF THE STALIN ERA

✿

STALIN'S years in power had been punctuated
by a series of purges, plots, bloodbaths, and
counterplots that brought not only death to millions but imprisonment, exile, and forced labor to tens of millions. The no-
torious system of prison/concentration camps needs no descrip-
tion here. At Stalin's death millions of victims of his false
accusations and trumped-up cases (e.g., the Doctors' Plot) were
still suffering in these camps and presented an immediate and
almost impossibly complicated problem to the new regime. Not
only must the innocent be given their freedom, they must be
given back their dignity, their status, their jobs, their former
lives—i.e., they must be "rehabilitated."

"Rehabilitation" is an especially important concept to keep in
mind in our discussion of Soviet political prisoners because the
implications are so far-reaching. More is involved than "making
amends." Rehabilitation implies innocence, and if the rehabilitated person is innocent, then those responsible for putting him
in a camp are guilty of abusing judicial procedure. Thus Presidium members could not simply wave a magic wand and release

and rehabilitate all political prisoners in one grand gesture because if certain cases were reopened the searchlight of inquiry would turn on themselves.

We should also not overlook the importance of "posthumous rehabilitation." What could this possibly mean to the deceased victim?

Under Stalin, the practice had been to evict from their homes the *families* of those declared guilty (especially if their apartments were desirable) and often to banish members of such families from the capital cities. They were forbidden to educate themselves for the military or diplomatic services nor could they hold any responsible position. (Queries about possible relatives under arrest were obligatory on any employment questionnaire.) After the rehabilitation of the convicted one—even posthumously—a family was entitled to return to its home city (for instance to Moscow or Leningrad) and was given a priority on waiting lists for an apartment there. Members were no longer stigmatized as "relatives of an arrested person" and widows of those who had died in the camps were granted special pensions.

We have seen how, after Stalin's death, Beria used a limited amnesty for minor criminals as an excuse to keep his own armed troops in Moscow. He also suddenly and unexpectedly ordered the release and rehabilitation of the physicians involved in the Doctors' Plot as well as the release and rehabilitation of a less well-known group of Georgian leaders arrested in 1952 in the Mingrelian Case. He certainly was not motivated by benevolence or a desire for personal popularity. The truth was that neither the Doctors' Plot nor the Mingrelian Case had been his idea. They had been concocted independently of the MGB at the initiative of Stalin, who then could accuse the MGB of a lapse in vigilance (for not having known about them) and move Beria away from the control panel of the terror machine. Thus after Stalin's death, Beria denounced the fabrication of the Doctors'

Plot and the Mingrelian Case and swiftly removed from power all those concerned in the prosecution of them.

His pronouncement was greeted with wild enthusiasm throughout the Soviet Union. The action was hailed as the beginning of a mass rehabilitation of all political prisoners.

But Beria proceeded cautiously. He "rehabilitated" a few carefully chosen individuals, basically persons related to highly placed government officials. Mme. Molotov, for example, was brought to Moscow directly from a camp, and Beria himself, together with her husband, met her. With the exposure of the bogus Doctors' Plot, Beria announced the release and rehabilitation of former MGB official Abakumov and of a number of other close friends, who were awarded responsible positions on the new MVD staff. Beria, of course, had no intention whatever of extending amnesty or rehabilitation any further since the last major terror operation immediately preceding the Doctors' Plot had been the so-called Leningrad Case in which he was very much involved (as was Malenkov) as we shall see.

The Central Committee, stunned by the implications of these "rehabilitations," adopted a resolution "On the Violation of the Law by the State Security Organs." This was indirectly aimed at Beria—"violation of the law" by the MGB was not limited to the Doctors' Plot. Furthermore, the "special privilege" aspect of rehabilitating those with proper connections turned the Committee's concern toward the millions of innocent people, victims of various waves of terror and purges, who were still left behind.

The courts were flooded with millions of appeals for review of the cases of people still in prisons and camps, or from others seeking posthumous rehabilitation for their relatives. The country's judicial apparatus could no longer rubber-stamp such requests with the standard "review denied." Insofar as practically the entire central administration of the NKVD/MGB was under condemnation, all of the cases of people arrested or convicted by this administration were open to question. The state prosecutor's office and the court system could not possibly handle the review of so many cases, nor could the government simply declare a general political amnesty. Some sort of selective criteria were needed, a definition of boundaries of what could be considered and what could not.

Khrushchev was of the opinion that the door should remain firmly closed to any rehabilitating of those vociferous opponents of Stalin (Zinoviev, Kamenev, Rykov, and Bukharin) who had been "openly" convicted at "open" trials, as it should remain closed to the restless ghost of Leon Trotsky. In these cases he believed Stalin to have been justified in liquidating those extreme "left" and extreme "right" elements that were undermining the fledgling communist state. He also thought that the ruthless collectivization of the peasant and the quashing of a part of the intelligentsia in the late 1920s and early 1930s had been justified. All of these repressions, not to mention the "glorious" traditions of the Cheka in the Civil War, were viewed as manifestations of the class struggle inevitable in any revolution.

But, in 1937–39 and later, thousands of prominent Party leaders, government officials, and military officers had been arrested, none of whom had ever been "dissident" or participated in any "opposition," who had always been faithful to the "general line of the Party," who had always voiced their devotion to Lenin and Stalin, and who had had brilliant revolutionary, administrative, or military careers. Here there was no attempt at "open" trials; they simply disappeared, in silence, unnoticed. Along with prominent Party members (secretaries of oblast committees, commissars, diplomats, and others), there were thousands of less notable, but similarly "pure" Party workers (secretaries of raion committees, factory directors, kolkhoz chairmen, and others), and ordinary citizens as well, Party members and nonmembers, scientists and scholars, workers and peasants—all sent to prison camps. Neither Khrushchev nor any of his colleagues in the Central Committee had any real notion of what the true scale of the repressions had been, but it was obvious that the question had to be faced.

Khrushchev and the Central Committee acknowledged that repression had smothered Party and state officials of their own generation, the elite of the late 1930s and 1940s, but they were reluctant to undermine the foundation of their own power, power that had been gained in a far from democratic manner. It is important to remember that Khrushchev, Kaganovich, Bulganin, and other luminaries of the Presidium had directly participated in the repression of others and, further down the ranks, many Party leaders had risen to their positions of leadership precisely by replacing those arrested and shot.

Although Khrushchev himself had not been above using terror techniques in 1937 when he was in the Ukraine, he was much more remote from the apparatus of terror than were his rivals in the Presidium, particularly Kaganovich, Malenkov, and Molotov. Khrushchev had not been the sponsor of any major political purge, whereas Malenkov was very closely linked with the Leningrad Case, as was Beria.

The Leningrad Case (1949–51), which destroyed the careers and personal lives of thousands of Party and state officials, was never directly mentioned in the Soviet press. Those arrested simply disappeared, and upon the subsequent appointment of others to their vacant posts, no explanation was offered as to how such prominent positions had become available.

According to official versions advanced much later, the chief intended victim in the Leningrad Case was a man second in command only to Stalin himself, Nikolai Voznesensky. He was the youngest and best-educated member of the Politburo and as First Deputy Chairman of the Council of Ministers and head of State Planning, he ranked higher in the government than did

Molotov, Kaganovich, Beria, or Voroshilov. Endowed with a quick, impeccably logical mind and considerable expertise in economics, he was regarded by the second-level echelon as the most likely successor to Stalin—which, of course, aroused Stalin's mistrust and resentment. Rumor had it that Stalin was particularly jealous of his achievements as an author. Voznesensky's *The Wartime Economy of the Soviet Union during the Patriotic War,* published in 1947, had been very well received. Its theoretical analysis of many aspects of socialist economics was beginning to be recommended along with the "works of Stalin" as a basic text in the study of Marxism. Although the book may have been a cause of Voznesensky's eventual liquidation where Stalin was concerned, it is more likely that his continually growing popularity made Malenkov, Beria, Molotov, and others jealous of his authority.

At the beginning of 1949, on Stalin's order, Voznesensky was "relieved" of all his duties—there were as yet no grounds whatever for his arrest. Merely to declare him an "enemy of the people" would not be enough.

At first Beria tried to implicate Voznesensky in the "loss" of some secret documents from State Planning files. He arrested several senior State Planning officials to get the necessary "testimony" from them. But the "confessing" officials could not prove Voznesensky's complicity and he was not arrested, while those who had "confessed" were convicted and sent off to prison camps. Some sort of more foolproof "case" had to be put together, and so one was manufactured by Beria and Malenkov.

According to charges made in the Leningrad Case, a number of officials of ministerial rank in the Russian SSR were conspiring to establish (in addition to the republic's Supreme Soviet and Council of Ministers) an independent Russian Communist Party and to make Leningrad the capital of the Russian republic with Moscow as the capital of the Soviet Union. Such a scheme of "greater Russian autonomy" was declared to be the work of "wreckers" whose aim was to weaken the central government, undermine the Party Central Committee, and thus attack Stalin, who stood at the head of each.

From the very top leaders down through the ranks, thousands of senior Party and government personnel were arrested including, of course, Nikolai Voznesensky and his brother A. A. Voznesensky, who was the Minister of Education of the Russian SSR. Capital punishment, abolished after World War II, was reinstated in the Criminal Code specifically for the Leningrad Case and the most prominent of the accused were shot.* The others were swallowed up by the concentration labor camps and were still there in 1953. It was obvious that all those convicted merited rehabilitation.

352,726/920/KHR

A review of a case basically followed standard judicial procedure, with the summoning of witnesses and counterwitnesses, the refutation of accusations by the presentation of new evidence, and so on. The review of a single case thus could take months—and there were millions of cases waiting to be heard. For anxiously waiting families and friends, the process was agonizingly slow. Of the 12 to 13 million people thought to have been in concentration camps during Stalin's time, only about 4,000 had been released in 1953, but even this small trickle from the Gulag archipelago was to have a great impact on subsequent events. Persons with influential political connections continued to be given prime consideration. Khrushchev himself arranged for the release of certain former aides and friends from his days in the Ukraine and his work during the war. The number increased to 12,000 in 1954–55, and they were a very special 12,000. The majority had in the past been influential people from Party and state apparat with extensive

* By "shot" we do not mean "executed by a firing squad." In the Soviet Union, a person sentenced to death is shot from behind by a single executioner who fires a bullet into his head while the two are walking in a special area of the prison.

connections, and their return to active political life altered the composition and thereby the atmosphere of the Party's higher echelons.

Mounting public demand made it inconceivable to delay any further the expected large-scale rehabilitation. Because existing judicial bodies were unable to review so many cases quickly, temporary judicial commissions were created and accorded full authority to rehabilitate those held as prisoners at their place of confinement. Exact statistics have not been released, but best-calculated estimates say that in 1956–57 about 7 to 8 million people were released and allowed to return to their homes. In addition, 5 or 6 million were posthumously rehabilitated, a fact which, as we have seen, had important consequences for the surviving members of their families.

This mass rehabilitation of millions of Stalin's victims had an inestimable impact on the psychological outlook of every think-ing person in the Soviet Union. Returning prisoners who had been rehabilitated had a number of advantages. Rehabilitated workers had to be reinstated in jobs appropriate for their ability and training even after years spent in a camp. The victims of the war years—former prisoners of war or those forcibly carried off to Germany—were on the whole granted amnesty without being rehabilitated. Of those arrested as far back as 1937–38, only 4 or 5 percent were still alive in 1956 and most of them were too old and broken to work. Military men who had been executed or who had died in the prison camps were, by a special order of Defense Minister Zhukov, considered martyrs and of a merit equal to those who had died at the front; their widows received monetary compensation and a special lifetime pension. Although thousands were not released (Russian soldiers who had been captured and then served in the German army during the war, nationalists from the Ukraine and Baltic republics, etc.), in the main the Gulag system was broken up.

In 1955, when relations with West Germany were "normalized," and thousands of German prisoners of war still in Soviet detention camps were released, an amnesty was also declared for Soviet citizens who had been convicted of various degrees of collaboration with German occupation forces, usually merely because they had worked—under coercion—either in Germany itself or in German-held territory.

Khrushchev's leading role in the release of political prisoners won him general popularity, but nevertheless two attempts were made on his life about this time.* Nothing about them ever appeared in the Soviet press. The first attempt occurred during a trip to Belorussia, the second and more serious during a 1956 visit on the *Red Ukraine,* a cruiser of the Black Sea fleet, docked at Sevastopol. The cruiser blew up only minutes after Khrushchev had left it upon completing his tour of inspection. These attempts were apparently closely linked to his unflagging sponsorship of a widespread rehabilitation of political prisoners and seemed to have been organized by people themselves involved in the repressions of the Stalin years. Their motives can perhaps further be explained by the following.

For very understandable reasons, many of those returning from the prisons and camps were not content with merely going home in meekness and gratitude. They sought some kind of retaliation, whether simple moral condemnation or formal legal action, against those responsible for their suffering—the ones who compiled false evidence, conducted the interrogations, tortures, and "trials," and who viciously participated in the carrying out of sentences. Of course many people had been involved, and a great number of them could still be found in prominent positions. Once more the Central Committee and the Procurator-General's office were flooded with petitions—this time concerning the complicity of senior officials still highly placed

* Information about these attempts was reported in *Politichesky dnevnik* (Political Diary), no. 3. Cf. *Politichesky dnevnik 1964–1970* (Amsterdam: Herzen Foundation Press, 1972), p. 15.

in the government hierarchy. A number of such accusations, accompanied by detailed evidence, leaked out through underground publications and aroused reactions of shock, panic, guilt, and anger.

It became known, for instance, that the then current Minister of Higher Education, V. Stoletov, had been directly responsible for the arrest and "liquidation" of many scientists and selection specialists in Saratov; that a member of the Central Committee and director of the Institute of Philosophy, M. B. Mitin, and the Soviet ambassador to China, P. F. Yudin (both of them Academicians) had brought about the arrest and liquidation of many distinguished scholars in 1936–38; and that Academician T. D. Lysenko had been linked to the arrests of many prominent geneticists. The chairman of the Writers' Union, A. Fadeev, had been directly responsible for the arrests of well-known writers. The list could go on and on.

It was of course necessary to investigate the charges although the process would take a long time, but no longer did anyone suddenly "disappear." Occasionally there could be a minor demotion or even self-condemnation (Stoletov, Minister of Higher Education of the Soviet Union, was dropped to the position of Minister of Higher Education of the Russian SSR; Fadeev, chairman of the Writers' Union, committed suicide), but on the whole the problem of accountability could not be resolved without a radical shake-up in the Party and government leadership. Khrushchev himself was not entirely without blame and the same was true of no small number of his associates. Unexpectedly, I. A. Serov, for a time head of the KGB, who had long been considered a personal friend of Khrushchev and who (as we shall see in chapter 7) had given him major support during the Molotov-Malenkov-Kaganovich "conspiracy," was dismissed in 1958. After the war Serov had directed a series of operations in the "liberated" countries of Eastern Europe and in Germany. Upon his dismissal, his apartment and dacha were searched and a large number of valuable works of art and other treasures, illegally appropriated from various collections in Germany and elsewhere, were confiscated. But, despite this, Serov was not arrested, but simply told to stay home. He continued to live with his family, apparently receiving a general's pension.

But still the millions of people who had survived but not forgotten the camps and who had now rejoined the mainstream of ordinary life, as well as the millions of others whose fathers, brothers, or husbands had been rehabilitated, became a major source of ferment in Soviet society and began to demand ironclad guarantees of due process of law and absolute safeguards against any possibility of a return to repression and terror. It was the activists in this group who called for more widespread denunciation of the crimes of the Stalin period, and who were to demand the publication of historical documents, access to NKVD and MGB records, and many other radical changes, to which neither Khrushchev nor his associates could accede.

chapter three

AGRICULTURAL
REFORMS

To understand why Khrushchev became popular so rapidly and how he strengthened his position in the Party hierarchy through major agricultural reforms, one must first have some background on the conditions that prevailed in agriculture at the time and come to grips with the intricacies of the Soviet agricultural system.

When farming was forced into collectivization in 1929, agriculture was divided into three types of productive/administrative units: sovkhozes, kolkhozes, and machine-tractor stations. The sovkhozes, formed from the large estates of former gentry landowners, were government controlled. They were in sparsely populated areas and, in 1929, constituted less than 5 percent of the land in agricultural use. Thus they were of relatively little importance on a national scale. Kolkhozes, according to their charters, were "voluntary" cooperative organizations of peasants and were directly answerable to the Communist Party. Each was run by an elected management who resolved problems through decisions reached by a general meeting of the kolkhoz members and not on the basis of directives from Party or state officials.

Sovkhozes were government farms and had full access to all the farm machinery they needed and could carry out the full farming cycle independently. Kolkhozes could purchase from the government only the simplest equipment, mainly tools for hand labor or crude plows for working with horses.

To complement the kolkhozes, the government established what it called "machine-tractor stations," with more sophisticated and complex equipment. These stations were supposed to service the kolkhozes under special contracts in exchange for produce, i.e., payments-in-kind from the crops harvested. Each machine-tractor station serviced several kolkhozes, taking over various farming operations. In 1929–32, when there was as yet little equipment available, the machine-tractor station did not make a major contribution toward food production since most farming was still dependent on work horses and hand labor. Over the years the importance of the stations grew and by 1953 they were doing most of the basic work that needed doing on a kolkhoz: plowing, sowing, cultivation, applying fertilizers, some harvesting with combines, hay-making, etc. Practically all the chores requiring modern equipment—tractors, combines, threshers, reapers, binders—were done by workers and drivers from the machine-tractor stations. This was a natural form of cooperation, since the kolkhozes had no technical facilities, repair shops, or people trained to use the equipment. The number of such stations increased steadily. In 1928 there were only 6; in 1932, 2,446; in 1940, 7,069. After the war some 2,000 additional stations were established.

One purpose of collectivization was to secure a reliable food supply. When Stalin introduced the kolkhoz system and drafted the first "kolkhoz model" statute the ideal was that the kolkhozes would produce stipulated amounts of food which the government would purchase for resale (in government-owned stores) in the cities and industrial compounds besides the payment-in-kind they owed for work on the land performed by the machine-tractor stations (also owned by the government). The government was not to expropriate but to purchase. The prices to be paid were set by the government, which also decreed the amount of produce that was due—a quota set regardless of whether a kolkhoz's actual output had been blasted by bad weather. Theoretically, after a kolkhoz had met its obligations, it would have surpluses, surpluses that would accrue to the kolkhoz and which could be distributed among its members according to the number of "workdays" a member had put in, or the surplus could be reserved for seed, or sold in city markets or in special stores. A kolkhoz would realize money from such sales.

But charges of payment-in-kind for tractors, combines, and other equipment were very high, while the prices the government paid to the kolkhoz were very low. Prices were in fact so low that they often did not even cover a fraction of the expenditures incurred in producing the crops!

Kolkhozes with good land and managed by shrewd chairmen could survive in this set-up. To further tip the scales, in a given raion or oblast the top leader always saw to it that there was at least one "model" kolkhoz (which got the major share of the fertilizer and machinery allotments, and hence the awards and bonuses or premiums for exemplary output). The majority of the kolkhozes not only did not have surpluses but piled up debts from year to year. Nonfulfillment of obligations in a given year, when there was, perhaps, a crop failure, incurred a responsibility to make up the deficit in the following year. In lean years, kolkhozes often had to deliver part of their seed reserves to the government, and then in the spring had to ask for assistance from their neighbors or from the government to sow their fields. Kolkhozes delivered milk from their dairies or meat to the government at similarly low prices, and thus there was no economic stimulus to develop cattle raising. In addition, government quotas were constantly being revised upward and determined not on the basis of the actual harvest, but by a theoretical "projected" harvest.

Stalin's psychology was simple if brutal. He thought that if a kolkhoz knew beforehand that the government demands would be large, then the kolkhozniks would work twice as hard to achieve a maximum harvest so that there would be something left for themselves. Unfortunately, Nature has her own laws and, without fertilizers, cannot assure an unending series of increase in yields. Since fertilizers were almost nonexistent, average yields in the Soviet Union did not increase from 1913 to 1953 and were only one-third of the yields in other European countries.

As provided by the kolkhoz statute, the family of a kolkhoznik had access to a small, so-called private, or "household" plot of ground for its personal needs. This was to be in exchange for work done on the kolkhoz (the plot was taken away from those who did not put in the requisite number of "workdays" per year). A family was allowed to keep *one* cow, a limited number of pigs or sheep, and some chickens and/or other poultry. The household plot could not be more than a quarter of a hectare (half an acre) in size.

These plots were not the exclusive property of the peasant but were subject to taxes both in money and payment-in-kind. Thus if a peasant family had chickens, it had to pay a certain number of eggs to the state as a tax; if it had a cow or pigs, it had to pay a tax in the form of milk and meat; if it had a garden or an orchard, it had to pay a tax in vegetables or in fruit. By 1940, the government was receiving from individual peasant plots 37.2 percent of the meat, 34 percent of the milk and butter, and 93 percent of the eggs that it received from the kolkhozes and sovkhozes as a whole.[*]

It is obvious that it is impossible to feed a family and livestock

---

[*] *Ekonomika sel'skogo khoziaistva* (Agricultural Economics), 1964, no. 9, p. 17.

on a quarter of a hectare of land. Nevertheless, it was these small plots which, both during the war and after it, became the primary source of food and general income for the individual peasant family. Peasants would cut hay to feed their livestock from remote meadows, in the woods, and similar places not used by the kolkhoz so that they could devote their small plots to fruits and vegetables, trying to achieve high yields through constant efforts to cultivate and improve the soil. During the war, when fruits and vegetables were scarce in the cities, produce from the kolkhozniks' private plots, sold in the markets at freely established and often quite high prices, became an important source of a city's supply.

As the "household" plot was granted only to those who worked on a kolkhoz, in the final analysis this "privilege" compelled the peasants to work kolkhoz land and supply labor for which they received virtually nothing. Underpaid labor on communal land was the condition on which they were allowed to have their own plots. This was in essence a state of semi-serfdom, which was reinforced by the stricture that a kolkhoznik was forbidden to move to the city or even to another district without the permission of the kolkhoz management and of the local soviet.*

Theoretically, the kolkhoz was an independent agricultural organization, and the state's interests in it were protected primarily through the Party structure. Important kolkhoz meetings were usually conducted by the secretaries or the instructors of the raion (district) Party committee. In agricultural raions, the Party committees were even more the masters than they were in urban or industrial raions, where executive committees of the soviets had some voice. Though it was possible to blame a local

---

* To live and/or work in a city or a town, a citizen had to get an internal passport for identification and police registration. Employing anyone without a passport was forbidden by law. Peasants had no passports, only identification papers from their kolkhoz or sovkhoz which did not entitle them to work any place else.

soviet for the inefficient operation of a small factory, or some ministry or other for inadequate achievement in some macro-industry, it was always the secretaries of raion and oblast committees who were held responsible for any shortcomings on the farms. The People's Commissariat on Agriculture had only a consultative function.

Collectivization caused a sharp drop in agricultural output in 1930–33, accompanied in southern regions of the Russian SSR and in the Ukraine by a famine during which several million people perished. Beginning in 1933 some improvement in output could be discerned, permitting better supplies to the rapidly growing cities as well as some export of grain, mainly to Germany.

The semi-feudal relationship between the peasants and the government assured the nation of its food supply both before and during the war, despite the drafting of millions of peasants into the army and the wartime loss of some 20 million people, of whom no less than 15 million were village residents. To this figure must be added some 10 million disabled veterans. The war in 1941–45, of course, inflicted enormous direct and indirect damage, particularly in the extensive regions under German occupation. In 1945, the nation's agricultural production was only 60 percent of its 1940 level.[*]

After the war, the government turned its back on agriculture and concentrated on rebuilding cities and restoring industry. Former peasants, especially young men just discharged from the army, did not rush to return to the semi-serfdom of the kolkhozes, but went instead to work in industry. Ironically as this development brought on a decline in the rural population it at the same time increased the need for a sharp rise in agricultural production to feed the urban one. With the onset of the

[*] *Narodnoe khoziaistvo v SSSR v 1964* (The National Economy of the Soviet Union in 1964) (Moscow: Central Statistical Administration [TsSU], 1965), p. 246.

cold war, food shipments from the United States came to a halt but, by then, the Soviet Union was committed to supplying food to several Eastern European countries as well as feeding itself.

From 1945 to 1953, however, agricultural development proceeded very slowly and by 1953 had reached only 104 percent of the 1940 level, with an urban population significantly larger than in 1940 and with greater exports of grain needed for Czechoslovakia, East Germany, and even China. Confronted with enormous difficulties in supplying the nonfarming populace with foodstuffs, the government was absorbing almost all the kolkhozes' output of grain and other products; the peasants were left with practically nothing from the harvest. They were forced to work for a meager income from the kolkhoz and could be arrested and sent to "corrective" labor camps for up to ten years for taking a sack of potatoes or wheat from the fields in which they themselves labored. Monetary and produce taxes on the household plots were increased as well, on kolkhoz and sovkhoz alike.

After 1946, agricultural taxes on household plots rapidly exceeded the point at which the peasant could consider intensive cultivation profitable. Fines and criminal charges were imposed for nonpayment of the taxes. But since the taxes were assessed not on the plot itself but on what was produced, the peasants not only stopped producing but destroyed what they had. First they chopped down their orchards, in order to avoid paying out money or fruit. Then they slaughtered their pigs and cows, and killed off their chickens. Potatoes became the principal crop on the household plots because the quota for potatoes was a reasonable one.

Behind this policy of confiscation there lay the theory that if the peasants were unable to feed their families from their plots, they would work harder on the kolkhozes and strive for better yields on kolkhoz land rather than on their personal plots. But the only result was that those who could possibly manage to do so left the farms altogether.

Despite the semi-feudal system of forced attachment of peasants to the land by refusing to grant them internal passports, there were still ways to escape kolkhoz life. Young people frequently simply did not join the kolkhoz, for, unlike the old days, there was no automatic registration of children who had attained majority. A master in the days of serfdom owned not only the peasant but his children as well. Kolkhozes, however, could hold only those who had formally enrolled. After military service, which in Russia has always been obligatory, Soviet youth did not return to the kolkhozes. For girls, there was the opportunity of higher education in the cities, the possibility of marriage, or the adventure of volunteering for work in some particularly distant and arduous region.

With no new people to work on the farms, agriculture had not long to survive and, in the course of two or three years, this could have brought on a catastrophe in food production and famine throughout the country. Stalin failed to realize this. Among those closest to him, only one man really comprehended the danger. That man was Khrushchev.

Stalin himself had no notion whatever of the specifics of agricultural production and harbored a particular animosity and mistrust toward peasants. He had never visited a kolkhoz village. State functionaries such as Zhdanov, Malenkov, Mikoyan, et al., understood even less than did Stalin, who had had a small garden during a three-year period of prerevolutionary exile in a Siberian village.

After 1948, Stalin's chief adviser in agricultural matters was T. D. Lysenko, a proponent of absurd notions of acclimatization and the alteration of the basic nature of plants and animals through environmental conditions. Under Lysenko's influence, the "Stalin Plan for the Transformation of Nature" was developed, consisting primarily of the creation of broad forest belts in the southern regions as protection against dry winds from the East. Stalin also proposed shifting southern crops to the north by "transforming their nature"; this led to unsuccessful attempts to grow oranges, lemons, olives, and even cocoa bean trees, for which enormous greenhouses were constructed. Agricultural regions received some funding and other assistance, but only for projects that either were ridiculous or would not improve conditions in a given region before twenty or thirty years had passed (e.g., the forest belts).

Khrushchev had been born into a peasant family and he was the only member of the Stalin Politburo who visited the countryside frequently, talking with kolkhoz directors and trying to familiarize himself with their problems. Perceiving the helpless condition of the smaller and poorer kolkhozes in particular, Khrushchev as early as 1949 proposed a rather bold project of combining or "consolidating" them, which was put into effect on a nationwide scale in the course of a year.

In 1929–30 collectivization had been achieved by having the peasants of each village join together in a kolkhoz. At the time, that was the only possible method of collectivization, since the agricultural equipment necessary for the establishment of more sizable farms worked by few hands did not as yet exist. Such markedly labor-intensive agriculture restricted small villages to the working of small areas. Thus a small kolkhoz was created from a small village, a medium-sized kolkhoz from a medium-sized one, and a large kolkhoz from a large one. In the south, where there were many large villages, several kolkhozes were sometimes organized from a single village.

In 1948–49 it was primarily the small and medium-sized kolkhozes that were collapsing from the state's excessive exploitation of the peasants. Large kolkhozes generally had better management, received greater assistance from the machine-tractor stations, and received credits and more attention from the raion administration. Realizing this, Khrushchev presented a plan to upgrade the small kolkhozes by combining them, or frequently by attaching them to a large neighboring kolkhoz in the same raion.

Peasants on the successful kolkhoz, much better off than their neighbors, usually resented having to share their resources with peasants on unsuccessful kolkhozes, which often were heavily in debt to the government. But merger was compulsory and very quickly all the small kolkhozes were absorbed. The total number of kolkhozes nationwide decreased by almost two-thirds. This reorganization forestalled the otherwise inevitable collapse of many small kolkhozes, which had previously had only 200 to 400 hectares of land for a few able-bodied kolkhoz members. It simplified kolkhoz administration by raion and oblast Party committees, permitted the selection of more capable kolkhoz chairmen, and improved the liaison between the kolkhozes and the machine-tractor stations of a given raion.

In each "consolidated" kolkhoz (sometimes comprising several thousand hectares and five to eight villages), Khrushchev also proposed the construction of a central settlement (an "agrotown"). This part of the project, already widely discussed in Party circles, was declared unsound by the Politburo, because there were neither the means nor the materials for the construction of such "agrotowns."

But consolidation alone was not enough and although it temporarily checked the crisis brought about by the ruinous exploitation of the small farms, the condition of peasant life continued to deteriorate. If previously things had been better in some villages, less good in others, and wretched in still others, within two to three years after consolidation the process of decline began to spread to the formerly prosperous villages that had had to share their resources with their less fortunate neighbors.

Much more than consolidation was needed, and Khrushchev was to propose a series of reforms, specifically aimed at helping the peasant, once he had the power to do so.

Primarily through his initiative in consolidating the kol-khozes, as well as his successful stand against Lysenko's attempts to replace high-yielding winter wheat with spring wheat in the Ukraine and the south (see chapter 5), Khrushchev gained the reputation of being the Man Who Understands Agri-culture. This contributed to his advancement to First Secretary of the Central Committee.

Upon becoming First Secretary, Khrushchev quickly proposed a sharp reduction of the produce taxes on household plots, and the abolition of taxes-in-kind on certain types of property (on fruit trees, cows, etc.). They would be replaced by monetary taxes based on the individual household as a whole in proportion to the number of people in the family. In addition the government would *purchase* from the peasants any surpluses at fairly high prices. This plan was quickly enacted into law by the Supreme Soviet in the summer of 1953. It immediately brought relief to the economic plight of the countryside and an improvement in the morale of the peasants who, for the first time in twenty-five years, felt that the governmental vise which had been squeezing them more and more had not only halted, but had even relaxed somewhat.

In September 1953 at a special plenum on agriculture held by the Central Committee, Khrushchev proposed, and the plenum agreed, that taxes on individual plots be reduced still further, that special benefits be provided for those peasant families who did not have a cow or other livestock for their own use, and that blue- and white-collar workers living in villages, small towns, and on the margins of cities to be encouraged to keep cows, pigs, and chickens, and to maintain gardens and small orchards without having to pay taxes on them. "We must abandon the pre-conceived idea that it's disgraceful for a blue-collar worker or a white-collar worker to have livestock of his own," Khrushchev declared at the plenum.*

Taxes on individual household plots were reduced once again, and the tax on having a cow or pigs was eliminated entirely.

This reform of Khrushchev's, which actually affected only the very small sector (in terms of area) of the household plots—hardly more than 2 percent of all land under cultivation—nevertheless produced rapid and dramatic economic results. The number of cows and other livestock owned by individuals rose. In 1953 almost a quarter of the 20 million peasant families did not have a cow; in 1959 virtually all peasant families had a cow and the number of cows owned by blue- and white-collar workers in small towns and suburban zones had increased to 3.5 million.† Within a few years the number of sheep had doubled; the number of pigs and poultry also increased sharply. Orchards flourished again. As early as 1954, the prices of farm products for private sale in the city markets went down. Tension in the countryside eased and the potential food crisis did not occur.

It was a sort of "New Economic Policy" in agriculture, benefiting a private sector of production, albeit a small one. This agricultural NEP involved a certain democratization, in that the government was not going to interfere in one area of people's lives, allowing them to decide for themselves what they would do with the quarter hectare of land they had received more or less on lease. Soon the desire to have a small piece of land for gardens and orchards spread even beyond the workers in small towns and suburbs. Institutions in large cities were permitted to

* N. S. Khrushchev, "O merakh dal'neishego razvitiia sel'skogo khoziaistva SSSR" (On the Means to Further the Development of Agriculture in the Soviet Union), speech at the Plenum of the Central Committee (Moscow: Gospolitizdat, 1953), p. 28.

† Narodnoe khoziaistvo SSSR v 1961g (The National Economy of the Soviet Union in 1961) (Moscow: Central Statistical Administration [TsSU], 1962), pp. 382–83.

seek plots of unused land in rural areas along roads, in the woods, and near railroad tracks, and to divide it among their employees for vegetable gardens and orchards, usually 1,000 square meters to a family. This was the beginning of so-called collective gardens for workers, where they could work for themselves after hours or on their days off.

The problem of the household plots could be resolved rather easily, for it did not require any elaborate financial or organizational measures. Although he relieved the situation of the tax-burdened peasants, Khrushchev could not, by this one gesture, improve the entire spectrum of agriculture. Above all, it was necessary to increase the supply of grain (which is not grown on household plots), to increase the yield of certain specialized crops, to raise production of feed for kolkhoz livestock, and to find solutions for a number of other problems, without which it would be impossible to develop industry.

Thus other reforms also emerged from the special plenum on agriculture of September 1953. Kolkhozes and sovkhozes were to receive a much greater return from the state for their products. An increase was put into effect across the board and particularly a substantial one for state purchases of meat and poultry (550 percent), milk and butter (200 percent), and vegetables (40 percent). The prices paid for any "surpluses" were also increased. All old debts were canceled.

Other reforms included a planned growth in production of fertilizer and agricultural equipment, the granting of credits for construction of dairy farms, an increase in wages for machine-tractor station workers, etc. These additional measures would show results in several years' time, but the raising of the prices paid for products had an immediate effect, since under the new arrangement the kolkhozes received considerable sums of money from the government and could pay the peasants for their work. The semi-feudal character of relations between the kolkhoz and its peasants was greatly changed.

It was also decided to make the kolkhozes more aware politically and to mobilize (to become chairmen, work brigade leaders, bookkeepers, Party organizers) some 20,000 to 30,000 experienced Party members, many of whom had an agronomic education. These workers were paid high salaries by the government for their first two or three years.

Such reforms had an unquestionably healthy effect on the development of agriculture. The production of grain, about 80 million tons in 1953, rose to 136 million in 1958. Of this 136 million, almost 60 million was delivered or sold to the state, almost twice as much as in 1953.* Area yield increased, on the average, from seven to eleven centners per hectare (one centner equals 100 kilos or 220 pounds). Meat production nationwide rose from approximately 6 million tons to 8 million (32 percent). The rise in milk production was 61 percent, of eggs 44 percent, of wool 36 percent. Sugar-beet production more than doubled.

Payments to kolkhozniks both in foodstuffs and cash totaled 134 billion roubles. At the present rate of exchange this was about $600 per year per peasant family.† Although this figure seems quite modest, it must be remembered that in 1953 a family had received the equivalent of only $150 from the kolkhoz.

With the increased income from personal plots taken into consideration, the material situation of the Soviet peasant, on the average, became almost equal to that of a lower-level Soviet industrial worker. An agricultural crisis seemed to have been averted and this unquestioned achievement was one of Khrushchev's major accomplishments, enhancing his political power and influence.

* *Narodnoe khoziaistvo SSSR v 1958g* (The National Economy of the Soviet Union in 1958) (Moscow: Central Statistical Administration [TsSU], 1959), p. 350.

† *Ibid.*, p. 367.

chapter four

THE CHALLENGE
OF THE WEST

KHRUSHCHEV had great imagination and soaring ambitions for the future. His dream was that the Soviet Union should lead the world—in industry, science, and the arts. The reason he concentrated so intensely on agriculture was that he knew that extricating the country from its cycle of chronic agricultural crises was essential to the success of any economic or political progress. Without an adequate supply of food and agricultural raw materials, neither light nor heavy industry could expand.

Under Stalin, grandiose technical projects, such as the construction of canals, dams, new cities in the north and Far East, factories, mines, even the new high-rise building of Moscow University, had all been carried out primarily through use of the slave labor of so-called convicts. Almost 15 percent of the most important scientific projects and not less than 50 percent of atomic energy research had been conducted in special MGB and MVD institutes by political prisoners who, in everyday life, had been distinguished specialists and scientists. For five or six years after World War II, millions of German prisoners of war also worked at various construction sites in different parts of the country.

Converting this forced labor system to one of normal industrial and scientific employment could not be achieved overnight, but nevertheless the process did begin after 1953. If normal industry and science were to replace peonage, it was necessary to build housing, to pay realistic wages to regular blue- and white-collar workers, and to ensure an adequate supply of foodstuffs, clothing, and recreational facilities. The relevant standard of comparison could no longer be the Russia of 1913, but rather conditions existing in contemporary Western countries.

A few steps toward this goal had already been taken—the first reforms of agricultural conditions and the rehabilitation of the political prisoners. The next step was to give reassurance that the old secret-police system of terror and repression would never operate in the same irreversible way again.

THE TRANSFORMATION OF THE MGB

Beria had not gone alone to his downfall. His top associates as well as the central staff of middle-level branches of state security, down to the heads of local administrative units, went down with him. But no serious measures were taken to punish rank-and-file participants of the Beria power structure. A number of old-time MGB workers were retired on pension. Younger ones were appointed to the security or personnel departments of special industrial and scientific compounds.

From the ashes of the old autonomous MGB/MVD arose the KGB, the Committee for State Security *at* the Council of Ministers. Government committees at that time were divided into two kinds: those which were committees *of* and those which were committees *at* the Council of Ministers. The preposition *at* (*pri*) indicated an "inter-departmental" committee that was actually subordinate to the Central Committee of the Communist Party and not to the Council of Ministers of the Soviet Union.*

A. N. Shelepin, head of the Youth League (Komsomol), was soon appointed KGB chairman; under his vigorous direction, the character of security personnel underwent a dramatic change. The majority of professional "Chekists" were removed and their posts, sometimes equivalent in rank to that of a general, were given to comparatively young men from the Moscow and oblast Komsomol organizations. Oblast and raion Komsomol committee members were entrusted with setting up KGB administrations at the oblast level. Even the problem of "ideological subversion from abroad" ("internal dissidents" had not as yet made an impression) was entrusted to a special section of the Central Committee.

The important point is that the new apparatus was no longer independent, subordinate only to a Stalin-like godhead. An oblast security chief now reported to the secretary of the oblast Party committee. In some raions, instead of separate sections for state security, small sectors were formed directly within the raion committee, and if it was necessary to have informers, they were recruited from among Party members directly by the raion committee. Along with its autonomy, the security apparatus lost the combined power to arrest, try and sentence, and execute. The KGB system could now only investigate and arrest; trial and sentencing became the province of the courts; the system of camps and prisons was supervised by the Ministry of Internal Affairs. This division of functions gave the Party a much more influential role as final arbiter when it came to decide the expediency of a proposed repressive measure. It soon was under-

---

* State Censorship (Glavlit) in the form of the "Committee for the Protection of State Secrets in Print *at* the Council of Ministers," the "State Commitee on Cinematography," and a number of others have the same status. Only financing for these committees originated in the Council of Ministers.

stood that no Party member, much less a Party administrative leader, could be arrested on a political charge unless his case had been reviewed by his local Party committee and a decision had been taken for expulsion from the Party.

Secretaries of oblast, city, and raion Party committees were in full charge within their own areas and the fear of sudden arrest disappeared at that level. Because of this reform, Khrushchev could now count on full support from oblast secretaries who, by the way, formed a majority in the Plenum of the Central Committee. The relationship between the Central Committee and the government of the Soviet Union at the top now paralleled the relationship between Party committees and executive committees at the oblast level. Directives to the government came from Khrushchev, and Khrushchev became the most influential leader not only in the Party, but in the country at large as well.

The extra-legal "special boards" (known as "troikas"), which formerly had existed within the security organs and which had authority to sentence in all cases under investigation by the old NKVD/MGB, were abolished. These "troikas" had more often than not paid no attention to any so-called Criminal Code or judicial procedure. Before 1953, the majority of regular courts handled only cases dealing with petty crimes, work-related offenses, divorce and civil cases, and so forth. Now these courts received broader jurisdiction, including political cases. But because these "people's courts" were not prepared in practice to consider and render judgment in political cases, the machinery that had in the past relentlessly delivered thousands of political prisoners to the camps automatically came to a halt. During the entire time that Khrushchev was in power, there was not one major new *political* trial of national scope.* Of course so-called

* Although the number of persons convicted for violations of politically centered articles of the Criminal Code was apparently not more than a few hundred during Khrushchev's time, the total number of political prisoners remained quite large. Khrushchev's rehabilitation policy did not extend to many categories that

anti-Soviet activity was still considered a crime and some groups of students and intellectuals were sentenced (for example, for protests against Soviet military suppression of the Hungarian uprising in 1956). Although in scattered areas in the provinces (but on the orders of the local committee, *not* on directives from Moscow) a certain number of political arrests doubtless occurred, political terror as an everyday method of government was replaced under Khrushchev by administrative methods of repression (expulsion from the Party, dismissal from the universities, loss of job, etc.).

A MODEST ACHIEVEMENT

Those persons maneuvering for power after Stalin's death had more to consider than a simple reorganization of the country's police system. In 1953, international relations were extremely tense. It was the hottest period of the cold war. The Korean War, begun in 1950, was sputtering on with no end in sight. Relations with Yugoslavia were strained to the limit and Stalin's old feud with Tito was still reflected in daily anti-Yugoslavia propaganda.

Khrushchev dealt with the latter problem quite successfully, displaying considerable expertise. Although his touch was not overly apparent in any rapid resolution of the Korean conflict, it was obvious in 1955, when Khrushchev and Bulganin reversed the Soviet Union's attitude toward Yugoslavia, arrived in Bel-

---

could be considered "political." In addition to the exceptions listed earlier, there were the active participants in nationalistic movements in the Ukraine and the Baltic republics in the years immediately after the war. Next, Khrushchev had had a law enacted regarding so-called "parasitism" under which it was possible to bring charges against young people who considered themselves to be poets or artists but who were not officially accepted as members of the Writers' or Artists' Union. Also under Khrushchev, the enforced hospitalization of "socially dangerous" "mentally ill" individuals was introduced, a procedure that absolved psychiatrists of legal responsibility for the improper commitment of people to mental hospitals.

grade and, to everyone's complete surprise, declared the tragic and enduring enmity to have been the result of Beria's infamous intrigues. Tito was all forgiveness and understanding and the Soviet Union found that it had reclaimed a friend. The news was very well received by the people back home.

Once Khrushchev took an interest in foreign policy and traveled abroad, he realized that Soviet agriculture and the economy in general were backward not only compared to the United States (which could be explained by historical factors) or Great Britain (which could be attributed to her exploitation of her colonies and former colonies), but also lagged behind West Germany, France, and even Japan, all of whom had achieved rapid reconstruction after the devastation of war. Of course it was impossible to duplicate a capitalist system, but Khrushchev challenged the nation to study the achievements of other countries, thus supplanting the old Stalin/Zhdanov doctrine of resisting "cosmopolitanism" and rejecting everything foreign; this new approach was extremely important for the development of Soviet science and technology and also made the government pay greater attention to the production of consumer goods.

Khrushchev did not have the scientific training or background to handle technological problems himself, but he would, for example, ask to see technical and general films about agriculture. There were screening facilities in the Kremlin and Khrushchev liked to show foreign films with simultaneous translation on technological and agricultural achievements abroad to top-ranking Soviet leaders. Afterwards special commentators (for agricultural films this was sometimes Lysenko) would provide further clarification of any points Khrushchev found unclear. Sometimes these films were then shown at technological or agricultural institutes and other organizations.

Starting in 1953–54, the Western influence began to penetrate many areas of the economy—construction, agriculture, and industry. Foreign industrial, agricultural, or general appliance exhibits opened regularly in the Soviet Union (the most famous was to be the American exhibition of 1959); almost all the items displayed were purchased afterwards as models for modernizing Soviet products, machinery, or other devices. On the whole this influence was a positive one. Khrushchev displayed inexhaustible energy in his attempts to introduce into the Soviet Union anything that would help to develop the nation's economy.

It would be difficult to enumerate all the innovations made at Khrushchev's direct suggestion or under the impact of what he discovered about or observed in the United States, Great Britain, the Scandinavian countries, and elsewhere. Many were beneficial and are still being applied.

For example, Khrushchev was responsible for the great expansion of housing construction. To expedite building, he ordered that new methods of prefabrication be used (entire rooms were made up in special assembly plants), a pragmatic decision but, for the same reason, he insisted on unnecessarily ugly standardized building plans and cut back specifications even for these. Apartment buildings were limited to four or five stories so that expensive elevators would not be needed. Balconies were also considered a superfluous luxury.* Blocks of such apartment houses, found throughout Moscow suburbs, were quickly labeled "Khrushchev slums." †

American-style cafeterias and self-service vending machines sprang up everywhere. (It had been this American way of

---

* In 1965–66 it was found that enough low-rise housing to accommodate all who needed it would cover too much ground and would make Moscow too large a city in area, that the necessary roads, gas, water, and heating supplies cost more than elevators. Since then, apartment houses within Moscow city limits must be at least 12 stories high. They have elevators, balconies, and airy, spacious rooms.

† The Russian word for such housing became *khrushchoby*, a punning combination of "Khrushchev" and *trushchoby*, the Russian word for slums or tenements. (Translator's note.)

speedy self-service eating that Ilf and Petrov had satirized back in 1935 in *One-Story America*.) Cybernetics, once declared a "bourgeois pseudo-science" under Stalin, was "rehabilitated," and computer technology and the utilization of computers in industry, science, and economics developed, although the time lag kept this technology considerably behind Western practice. In agriculture, a start was made in shifting from outmoded "hitched" agricultural attachments drawn by the tractor to "hinged" implements mounted directly on the tractor, allowing one driver to perform several tasks without an assistant. Road construction expanded and a number of highways, comparable to Western superhighways, were built.

Khrushchev well understood that he would be judged by ordinary citizens not only on the basis of greater production of coal, oil, or steel, or even in terms of his political reforms or foreign policies—to win approval he would have to raise substantially the low standard of living of the great masses of people. But to achieve all his ambitions, Khrushchev had to consolidate his power and, although his popularity was growing daily, there were those around him who were antagonistic, indeed who even wanted power for themselves.

The nucleus of the Presidium of Central Committee was, for various individual and collective reasons, against Khrushchev's "radical ideas" in the political realm. Even Khrushchev's faithful opponents, Malenkov, Molotov, and Kaganovich, had no real notion of the agricultural situation, feared "sweeping" reorganization, and were totally uninterested in any political housecleaning beyond the simple liquidation of the Beria "Set."

We have seen how those who had managed to survive the Stalin years had rid themselves of Beria. Now let us observe the maneuvering for power among Kaganovich, Malenkov, Molotov, and Khrushchev, a struggle that began many years before 1953.

chapter five

THE POWER STRUGGLE

THERE could no longer be any doubt about the extent of Khrushchev's influence over top-level decisions after his decisive contribution in initiating major political and economic reforms; but in 1954 there was still no single designated leader. And the principle of "collective" leadership, declared after Stalin's death, still prevailed. For twenty-five years the Stalin cult had dominated people's minds—Soviet citizens were taught to believe that only the "Great Father of the People" could single-handedly deal with all the complexities involved in governing a nation and directing foreign policy. Therefore the only possible alternative to his supreme wisdom was the collective effort of his leading comrades and disciples, who now had to close ranks around the memory of the Teacher. During Stalin's lifetime, none of his associates had been especially admired by intellectuals or the academic/scientific/economic community. All of those who had begun to distinguish themselves and gain influence as a result of service to others, organizational talents, notable achievement, or an ability to deal with economic problems in an efficient and businesslike way had, for one reason or another, "disappeared" from the political arena by 1953. In 1954 only one of Stalin's Old Guard could still be found within the collective leadership—Marshal Zhukov, who had been forced into retirement by Stalin but was now restored as Deputy Minister of Defense.

In his climb to the top of the Kremlin pyramid, Khrushchev had to pass by several human obstacles, some of them a greater challenge than others. Molotov, as Chairman of the Council of People's Commissars until 1941, had risen high in the prewar years. Now he considered his position in the Party to be insufficiently influential and so sought to keep Khrushchev away from the area of foreign affairs. Voroshilov, saddled with the blame for involving the Soviet Union in a war with Finland in 1939 without vital intelligence information about Finland's defense lines and castigated for his poor command of the southern front in 1941, which had led to Nazi Germany's initial quick victory over the Red Army in the Ukraine, could not forget that it was Khrushchev who, as a member of the Military Council for the Southern Front, had pushed for Voroshilov's removal from any kind of military authority. The bitter feelings that existed between Khrushchev and Kaganovich dated back to 1947 and those between Khrushchev and Malenkov back to 1949.

Stalin had always considered Khrushchev a properly devoted and subservient functionary and even felt slight twinges of good-will toward him. For this reason he stubbornly had not dismissed Khrushchev from the old Politburo or from the Presidium of the Central Committee, despite the frequent urgings of Kaganovich and Malenkov to do so.

The first serious attempt to demote Khrushchev had been in March 1947 when Khrushchev was accused of not being sufficiently vigilant in stomping out nationalist agitations in the Ukraine. He was "relieved" of his post as First Secretary of the Central Committee of the Communist Party of the Ukraine. Kaganovich was dispatched from Moscow to take his place and to establish "law and order." Khrushchev, who was also Chairman of the Council of Ministers of the Ukraine, retained this governmental post and his membership in the Politburo but, in the Ukraine, where he had previously been in full control and a quite popular leader, he was now subordinate to Kaganovich.

The appointment of Kaganovich was only partly connected with "nationalism," although it was felt that Kaganovich, as a Jew, would be more ruthless in eliminating Ukrainian nationalist tendencies. The main reason Kaganovich was sent to the Ukraine was to serve as a "strong arm" in putting down any sign of disturbances over a famine which threatened the area after the severe 1946 drought (the worst since the devastating drought of 1891). In 1932, it had been the Ukraine which had suffered most from a famine caused by a crop failure, collectivization, and too-high state taxes that had to be paid in grain just after the harvest; more than 2 million Ukrainians had died of starvation at that time, and the bitter memory of this tragedy was still alive.

A dispute over the superiority of spring or winter wheat became the theoretical point at issue in the political conflict between Kaganovich and Khrushchev, and in this conflict Khrushchev displayed considerable determination and courage, despite the risk to his own career. In the postwar period, when the threat of famine was again a dominant issue, an individual's views on agricultural policy could assume great significance in determining his position in the Party hierarchy.

In 1947, a sizable expansion of acreage sown in spring wheat was planned for the Ukraine at the expense of acreage planned to be sown in winter wheat. This recommendation was part of a pet scheme of T. D. Lysenko, President of the Academy of Agricultural Sciences, who derived his notion of the superiority of spring wheat from the purely theoretical constructions of the "grass-rotation system of cultivation," propounded by the agronomist V. Vil'yams. Khrushchev clearly understood this project's shortcomings and its hazards for his homeland. For the Ukrainian peasant, winter wheat was a more traditional and reliable crop than spring wheat. Spring wheat was customarily sown mainly as a reserve in case the winter crop would be badly damaged by unfavorable weather.

In the Ukraine and southern Russia in general, winter wheat gave, on the average, a one and a half to two times higher yield, and was also less sensitive to periodic dry spells. Winter wheat, sown in early autumn when there is adequate moisture in the soil, manages during the fall to grow a sizable grass vegetative mass; in the spring, when again there is ample soil moisture, it quickly shifts to reproductive growth and matures in midsummer. Thus, a *summer* drought, frequent in southern regions, has little effect on the yield, and the longer period of grass vegetative growth (from autumn to the middle of the following summer) ensures a greater number of reproductive stems growing from a single seed and a higher yield per amount of seed grown.

Spring wheat yields a more valuable so-called "hard" grain with a higher protein content, but since it is sown in the spring, its reproductive development begins in midsummer, with maturation starting at summer's end. Summer droughts, even mild ones, decrease yields sharply; severe droughts ruin the crop entirely. For this reason, expansion of spring wheat in the Ukraine was an extremely risky and unpopular undertaking.

Nevertheless Kaganovich insisted on a rapid expansion of spring sowings, Lysenko supported this project from the "scientific" point of view, and the agricultural section of the State Planning Commission (Gosplan), headed by V. S. Dmitriev and his deputy S. T. Demidov, demanded that stipulated levels for spring wheat planting be met.

The dispute over wheat quickly erupted into political conflict and in the summer of 1947 rumor had it that Khrushchev had lost his government job in the Ukrainian Republic as well as his Party one. However, Kaganovich failed in his attempts to remove Khrushchev in toto, and his plans for dealing with the nationalist Ukrainian intelligentsia also met resistance and were abandoned for fear of inspiring even stronger nationalistic feeling. It is interesting to note that the Ukraine's MGB apparatus was to a large extent saturated with Khrushchev supporters and Kaganovich, an outsider and government man from Moscow, was unable, in a short time, to form a coterie of his own. Kaganovich's Jewish origin also apparently was a handicap, for anti-Semitism, almost openly encouraged by Stalin after the war, traditionally had its strongest roots in the Ukraine and not in central Russia.

By making skillful use of the situation and adroitly playing all angles, Khrushchev managed to hold on and by the end of 1947, Kaganovich was recalled to Moscow, having lasted in the Ukraine less than a year. Khrushchev reassumed the post of First Secretary of the Ukrainian Party. Soon after, at a major conference of Ukrainian scientists and agricultural specialists, he received full vindication—it was conclusively proved that winter wheat gave a higher yield. To avoid taking the blame for making faulty recommendations, Lysenko in an article entitled "On the Agronomic Theory of V. R. Vil'yams," declared that Vil'yams' opinions about the superiority of spring wheat for the Ukraine were mistaken.* As Vil'yams had been dead since 1939, it was a simple matter to shift all responsibility to him.

In 1953, as soon as Khrushchev became First Secretary of the national Party, he ousted Demidov and Dmitriev from State Planning. Ridding himself of Kaganovich was more difficult but disapproval was expressed in a symbolic gesture. The Central Committee had passed a resolution banning the time-honored custom of naming cities or institutions after living prominent Party leaders. The ban was retroactive. Several small towns and villages called "Kaganovich" had their former names restored,

* *Pravda*, July 15, 1950.

and in Moscow, the subway system, named in honor of Kaganovich in 1935, was now called the Lenin subway. However, in deference to Kaganovich's sponsorship of the construction of the subway, the Moscow City soviet settled on a compromise, renaming one of the stations, the former Okhotny riad (Traders' row) station in the center of the city in honor of Kaganovich. But because the name "Kaganovich station" gave no idea of location to passengers, the old name Okhotny riad was very soon restored until a few years later when the street was renamed Karl Marx Prospect and the subway station renamed along with it. The industrial city of Molotov in the Urals recovered its old name of Perm, and Voroshilovgrad in the Ukraine once more became Lugansk. No sizable cities or institutions had ever been named for Malenkov or Khrushchev and so the reputations of these two major figures could not be damaged by such a simple maneuver.

The friction between Khrushchev and Malenkov did not originate in their struggle for power after Stalin's death, but had begun several years earlier, again over Khrushchev's agricultural policy. Although Stalin had reserved for himself the role of absolute dictator in almost all areas of domestic and foreign policy, he was clearly unqualified, particularly after the war, to deal with agricultural problems. Yet this was the area of the economy to which, after collectivization, Stalin's prestige was most closely tied. Agriculture was unique in that failures could not be covered up by falsifying statistics; a shortage of foodstuffs was felt more keenly by the populace than was a shortage of coal, steel, or petroleum; some 80 percent of the total output of consumer goods by light industry depended on supplies of agricultural raw materials—cotton, wool, flax, animal fats, and so on. Thus, the Politburo member who could handle agriculture could count on a major role in running the country.

In December 1949 Stalin recalled Khrushchev to Moscow, where he became Secretary of the Moscow oblast and city committee and a Secretary of the Communist Party. He was also given control of the agricultural sector of the economy—which had interesting implications. By this time, Nikolai Voznesensky, formerly Stalin's second in command, had been arrested (the Leningrad Case) and Malenkov who, with Beria, had carried out this "operation," now occupied that dangerous position. It is not impossible that because of this overconcentration of power in Malenkov's hands, Stalin decided to grant almost equal weight to Khrushchev, assigning industry to Malenkov and agriculture to Khrushchev.

Khrushchev's first successful project was, as we have seen, the amalgamation of the kolkhozes. This, however, he considered only the beginning of a real rural modernization and of an alleviation of living conditions in the villages. He next advanced his plan for the establishment of central settlements of kolkhoz-towns (agrotowns) in the consolidated kolkhozes.

The project of creating "agrotowns" was doubtless utopian in 1951 on an all-Union scale, although just such a radical shift of investment from industry to agriculture could have rescued agriculture from its desperate situation. But Stalin was not prepared for such a sweeping change, and had been misled by a system of calculating harvests based not on actual output but on an artificial system of collecting and measuring field samples made before actual harvesting took place. This permitted falsification of productivity figures and the resultant increase in norms for deliveries to the state gave an illusion of prosperity in the cities while the countryside was rapidly running to ruin.

Malenkov seized his opportunity to discredit Khrushchev and declared the "agrotown" plan a dangerous and pernicious economic blunder. Stalin and Beria agreed, and the "agrotown" project was consigned to oblivion. A redistribution of responsibilities again put Malenkov in charge of agriculture, but he still could not force Khrushchev out of the Politburo altogether. He nevertheless continued his attack. As First Secretary, he circulated a "confidential" letter within Party organizations sharply condemning the idea of "agrotowns" and, at the Nineteenth Party Congress in 1952, delivered the General Report, where he again criticized Khrushchev's plan.* In the same report, Malenkov declared that the grain problem in the Soviet Union had been completely solved! After Stalin's death, simply by revealing the actual figures (grain output per capita in the Soviet Union in 1952 was lower than it had been in Russia in 1913), Khrushchev was able to vindicate himself and cast a shadow over Malenkov's reliability. But discrediting Malenkov's agricultural policy alone was not enough to unseat him as Chairman of the Council of Ministers.

To an outside observer, Malenkov's removal was not an absolute prerequisite for bettering the welfare of the country. He was not inferior in political acumen to any of the other members of the Presidium and, had he been able to act as part of a team, he might have been a beneficial check on the overly impetuous Khrushchev. Concentration of total power in one person's hands, bordering on authoritarianism, is always hazardous, especially in a country lacking democratic traditions. But, precisely because of this lack of democratic tradition, reciprocal distrust between the two leaders inevitably led to open conflict and to forcible removal of one by the other. Each believed that stability in government could be maintained by placing in key posts only those who were loyal and devoted to himself, and not through constitutional guarantees.

It was then just a matter of who was to go and recent events had given Khrushchev considerable advantage.

After Beria's execution in December 1953, a review of the Leningrad Case began. In the course of rehabilitation of its victims the prosecution also accumulated evidence implicating Malenkov, who had at the time gone to Leningrad, along with

* *Pravda,* October 6, 1952.

Beria, to direct the "investigation." A former assistant of Malenkov's, M. Andrianov, who had actively participated in organizing
the Leningrad Case and who had then been made First Secretary of the Leningrad oblast committee, had already been removed by Khrushchev in November and was now under investigation.

As a former co-participant with Beria, Malenkov could escape
total disgrace only with Khrushchev's sanction and then only at
the price of resignation. He relinquished the chairmanship of
the Council of Ministers at the end of 1954, but the official announcement was postponed, as was proper according to "democratic" procedures, until the regularly scheduled session of the
Supreme Soviet in February 1955. This to a certain extent preserved the government's reputation for methodical procedure in
the eyes of the world. Malenkov himself explained the reasons
for his resignation—his long career devoted to the Party left him
insufficiently experienced in government matters; he also took
direct responsibility for the poor management of agriculture
during 1950–53. Because of his voluntary resignation from the
Council of Ministers, Malenkov could retain his membership in
the Presidium of the Central Committee, but he no longer exercised any real power, and he was to remain in the background
until he once more entered the power race, as we shall see in
chapter 7.

The formation of a new Council of Ministers was entrusted to
Bulganin, a friend of Khrushchev's since prewar days. Two
Khrushchev supporters were appointed to head the agricultural
ministries (Procurements and Agriculture) in the new government. The former Minister of Sovkhozes, A. Kozlov, who had
backed Malenkov against Khrushchev, was dispatched to the
northern Caucasus to direct a single sovkhoz. Marshal Zhukov
became Minister of Defense, which at once gave the Army
needed weight and prestige in the government. Other Khru-

shchev protégés were also given key positions in the government and the Party apparat. Only after all these changes came about, taking nearly two years after Stalin's death, could it be said that Khrushchev had indeed achieved power on a national scale.

chapter six

AGRICULTURAL "MIRACLES"

PRODDED by Khrushchev, the Central Committee had taken a few cautious steps to provide the legislation necessary for a gradual improvement of agricultural conditions, but the poor harvest of 1953 and the shortages of the fertilizers, fodder, and machinery needed to guarantee any improvement in the following year forced Khrushchev to consider more dramatic methods. What was needed was a significant rise in agricultural output. The shortage of food products was so acute that even a 10 percent annual increase would have little effect on the food supply for the cities, particularly because urban populations were increasing so rapidly.

The concentration on industrial development and the expansion of transportation and communication created a situation where even the formerly self-sufficient villagers (peasants had ground their own grain, baked their own bread, processed their own dairy products, and butchered their own livestock) now traveled to nearby cities or industrial towns to buy bread, butter, and meat. In lean years when crops were poor and the government nevertheless requisitioned produce from the kolkhozes without considering local needs, kolkhozniks had to buy their foodstuffs in the cities or receive food parcels from friends or relatives in the cities. Almost every country family had relatives, friends, or former neighbors in the towns. Measures to restrict this practice (a ban on mailing food parcels from larger cities, etc.) had no effect. A situation arose whereby the city was feeding the countryside! The government could no longer concern itself with feeding only the urban population. The self-sustaining farmer ceased to exist and food came to be regarded merely as a commodity to be sold on the general state market for the whole population.

In an industrial country, food must be available in sufficient quantity and accessible to all; the Soviet Union could achieve this only through years of carefully planned development. To reach the levels of Western Europe or the United States, grain production would have to double, meat production triple, and poultry and egg production increase four to five times. The return to Russia's traditional role as an exporter of agricultural products would require an agricultural miracle. In this period the problem of agricultural production became not only a major domestic issue, but also an essential component of an active foreign policy aimed at enhancing Soviet ascendancy in the developing countries (India, the Arab world, Africa, Indonesia). Impoverished nations emerging from colonial dependence formed an important link in the expansion of the socialist sphere of influence.

A steady but slow growth of agriculture (along with fluctuations due to weather conditions) did not fit in with plans for an aggressive foreign or domestic policy and so, in 1954, Khrushchev began a dynamic reorganization of the traditional agricultural structure: first, by rapidly opening up millions of hectares of virgin and fallow land in the east and southeast; and second, by promoting corn as a major grain and fodder crop.

A NEW FRONTIER: THE VIRGIN LANDS

In September 1953, when the Central Committee special plenum on agriculture was in session, it was already apparent that the 1953 harvest would be a poor one. In fact, the overall grain output was less per capita than it had been in 1913, and state procurements of commodity grain were about 36 million tons, 2.5 million tons less than in 1940. Since there was no way to rapidly increase yields on poorly fertilized, over-used land, Khrushchev quite naturally turned to the possibility of expanding the acreage of sown land. It was clear that only by putting whole new areas under cultivation could there be quick results.

The virgin lands program was originally drafted as a temporary measure, a stopgap to gain time while the traditional food-producing areas were developed to full capacity through the use of modern fertilizers and the latest technical equipment. At that time, the Soviet Union still had vast tracts of unused or underused land suitable for agriculture. In Kazakhstan and the eastern regions of the Russian SSR alone there were more than 40 million hectares of virgin and fallow land, hayfields, and grazing land. To begin full-scale development of these regions in 1954 required immediate action. In January Khrushchev proposed a nationwide campaign. On his recommendation, the Seventh Congress of the Kazakhstan Communist Party adopted a resolution to begin large-scale development of Kazakhstan's virgin lands. A conference of machine-tractor station workers held in Moscow in February gave full support to the virgin lands program. And in March 1954 the Plenum of the Central Committee adopted a special resolution whereby not less than 13 million hectares of new land were to be put into cultivation. Approximately 20 million tons of grain were expected from them by 1955.[*]

* KPSS v rezoliutsiiakh. . . . (The Communist Party of the Soviet Union in Resolutions), part 3 (1954), p. 661.

During the spring and summer of 1954, a major nationwide organizational effort began. Through the recruiting tactics of Komsomol organizations, 300,000 volunteers set out for northern Kazakhstan, the Altai, and the southern regions of Siberia and the Urals. Migration, not only from the countryside, but from the cities as well, was encouraged. Special trains, carrying thousands of families, were dispatched to the new regions. Hundreds of settlements, temporary cities of tents, as well as roads, warehouses, storing facilities, and repairing equipment were built. Hundreds of gigantic new sovkhozes were established, some of them allotted tens of thousands of hectares of land at once. Almost all the new agricultural equipment coming off factory assembly lines was shipped to these regions. Some 50,000 tractors (as calculated in the traditional fifteen horse-power units), more than 6,000 trucks, and other mechanical equipment were shipped to the sovkhozes and to the machine-tractor stations serving the kolkhozes in the new regions.*

Directives for assimilating the virgin lands (beginning with 13 million acres) were already overfulfilled in 1954—some 19 million hectares were plowed,† and in 1955, an additional 14 million hectares were plowed. The breaking of ground in 1954, however, did not mean that all these tracts were sown with wheat. In the spring, sowing took place on a limited number of tracts, with plowing (mostly in steppe regions) continuing throughout the summer and early autumn in preparation for the 1955 sowing. The 1954 harvest was a good one, and the na-

* For reasons of statistical simplification, tractors were classified according to traditional (i.e., 1930–1940) 15 horsepower units. Under this system a modern 60 horsepower tractor was registered as *four* 15 horsepower ones. *Razvitie sel'skogo khoziaistva SSSR v postevoennye gody* (The Development of Agriculture in the Soviet Union in the Postwar Years) (Moscow: 1972), p. 145.

† *Narodnoe khoziaistvo SSSR v 1956g* (The National Economy of the Soviet Union in 1956) (Moscow: Central Statistical Administration [TsSU], 1957), p. 127.

tion's total grain output increased by 10 million tons *—but the greater part of this increase came from the old agricultural regions. Breaking in of the virgin lands was still only beginning and as yet very little was harvested there—no more than 3 million tons. Hopes for the new regions were focused on 1955.

These hopes were dashed when 1955 turned out to be a very dry year for the eastern part of the country. Almost all the spring wheat sown in the virgin lands perished. Living conditions during the winter were rigorous and supplies of foodstuffs and other goods were unreliable and inadequate. Therefore thousands of people who had moved to these regions on a permanent basis now began to leave. For Khrushchev this was an enormous failure and a bitter disappointment. Malenkov, Kaganovich, and Molotov criticized him openly for a rash venture employing "great leap" methods. It was suggested that if only all that had been fruitlessly invested in the virgin lands during the previous two years had been put to use in the traditional agricultural regions (the central zone, the Ukraine, the northern Caucasus, and the Don and Volga regions), the results would have been very different indeed. Central Committee opposition hardened and members demanded that the "pointless" flow of equipment and manpower to the east be shifted to the west and south.

Khrushchev's grip on his place in the Central Committee became uncertain. However, he not only maintained his enthusiasm and support for the virgin lands program but demanded an even greater expansion of acreage. Thus 1956 was the decisive year both for the virgin lands program and for Khrushchev himself. A repetition of 1955's poor harvest would make Khrushchev's removal from office practically a foregone conclusion.

But 1956 turned out to be an exceptionally abundant year in the virgin lands. That summer, there was a healthy rainfall in

* *Ibid. 1958g* (pub. 1959), p. 436.

the east, while in the western regions there was a drought. At this time the virgin lands had little need of fertilizers since there were still substantial reserves of nutritive substances in the soil. The yield of wheat was unprecedented in the history of Soviet agriculture. Khrushchev, victorious, toured the region by car, plane, and helicopter, and hundreds of Party leaders visited the area. In the eastern regions alone, 63 million tons of grain were harvested. In the Soviet Union as a whole approximately 125 million tons were gathered, the largest amount in the entire history of the country up to that time, with more than half of that figure coming from the new regions. Kazakhstan alone harvested about 16 million tons—more than the entire Ukraine. Had it not been for the virgin lands, 1956 would have almost been a year of famine for the Soviet Union.

The bumper crop was a major triumph and vindication for Khrushchev and temporarily silenced his critics. Unfortunately, the unexpectedly large harvest created its share of problems. Even with the rapid dispatching of combines and other equipment from the western regions, it was impossible to harvest the entire crop before winter came and much grain was lost. Not all the grain that was harvested could be properly stored, as there were not enough storage barns and sheds. Not all the grain that was stored could be transported to where it was needed, as there simply were not enough trucks, roads, or manpower or, if by rail, there were not enough railroad cars properly equipped to carry grain and much grain was lost in transit. But these were all problems created by success and not by failure, and euphoria over the possibility of achieving an "agricultural miracle" was too strong for attention to focus on shortcomings. It seemed that at last some of the country's agricultural woes were behind it. These remote areas were underpopulated, and so the young new sovkhozes could not plan on diversified cultivation but only on a single-crop cultivation of wheat with a seasonal transfer of manpower from the western cities as temporary labor. It was ex-

pected that the task of full assimilation and settling of these
regions could take many years. Thus Khrushchev devised a special plan for the traditional agricultural regions—the central
zone, the Ukraine, the northern Caucasus, and the Don and
Volga areas.

THE CORN CAMPAIGN

If the opening of the eastern regions was intended as a solution of the grain problem, the production and determined promotion of corn as a fodder crop was intended as a solution of the
livestock problem. Khrushchev realized full well that the Soviet
Union had to increase its output of livestock as well as its output of grain. Only the traditional agricultural regions could be
relied upon to achieve this goal and lack of fodder was the chief
obstacle to the development of animal husbandry in these areas.
Khrushchev knew that in the United States corn was the principal feed crop and that livestock production flourished there
because of superior yields of corn. Since 1955, the post of "agricultural attaché" had been established in Soviet embassies and
through this channel a great deal of information and proposals
for change were directed to the Central Committee. In addition,
agricultural delegations and group excursions were sent to the
United States and other countries.

The great hopes placed on corn in past years had not been
realized. In the 1930s, the enormous success of corn genetics in
the United States and the shift to the general use of very high-
yield inbred-line hybrids, which greatly increased U.S. corn output, became the subject of sharp debate between the Lysenko
group and the classical school of geneticists, headed by N. I.
Vavilov. Vavilov considered the U.S. success in increasing corn
yields to be the most cogent demonstration of the practical value
of genetics and he proposed the introduction of this method into
the Soviet Union and the expansion of corn acreage in the

south. Lysenko dismissed the new methods of seed corn production as commercial propaganda put out by capitalist firms and held inbred-line hybridization to be injurious to a plant's "biology." *

In September 1953 Khrushchev proposed a significant increase in corn acreage for grain in the Ukraine and the south and for silage elsewhere. Nationwide silage procurements were insignificant and corn, at the so-called "milky-wax" stage of maturity, could be a very valuable silage crop not only in the south, but in the central zone as well.

The contemporary method of producing hybrid seed corn based on cross-line strains requires time, for pure inbred lines can be achieved only after several years of artificially induced self-pollination. To speed things up, a number of pure strains for specialized breeding were imported from the United States and special seed farms were established to produce hybrid seeds. Even then the whole program could not proceed as rapidly as Khrushchev wished. Furthermore, despite intensive propaganda promoting the virtues of corn, corn planting in the Soviet Union increased very little. On farms where corn was until then unknown, the new crop was approached with caution, and only small trial plots were planted, sometimes no more than a hectare. One reason for this reluctance was that there was no special equipment available and much of the labor had to be done by hand.

Khrushchev's great partiality for corn and especially for hybrid corn was quickly exploited by the Vavilov geneticists to weaken Lysenko's influence in the agricultural sciences. Khrushchev at this time did not show any special regard for Lysenko but rather, perhaps, remembered their clash in 1947 over the question of winter wheat vs. spring wheat. Lysenko's refusal to accept the superiority of hybrid corn in the past had

* For details see Zhores Medvedev, *The Rise and Fall of T. D. Lysenko* (New York: Columbia University Press, 1969).

forced the Soviet Union into purchasing large quantities of seed corn from the United States. Under constant fire, Lysenko was removed from his position as head of the Lenin Academy of Agricultural Sciences.

The small increase of corn acreage in 1954 did not please Khrushchev. And although the necessary seed, fertilizer, machinery, silos, and experience were lacking, the Central Committee, at Khrushchev's insistence, issued a directive that corn acreage was to be substantially expanded in almost all agricultural oblasts. This meant a cruel setback to the eagerly awaited newly adopted system of agricultural planning whereby kolkhozes would be permitted to decide for themselves what crops to raise. They were now ordered to plant corn, corn, and more corn. At every possible meeting or conference, Khrushchev hammered away about corn, recalling how potatoes had to be introduced into Russia by force in the eighteenth century. As a result of this pressure, the amount of corn planted (to be used as grain silage, and fodder) shot up dramatically, reaching some 18 million hectares.[*]

Although corn was by no means a success everywhere, the relatively hot summer of 1955 (with drought in the southeast) was beneficial. Even on farms in the central zone and the Baltic republics, corn had a high yield for silage and, in the south, procurements not only of silage corn but of grain corn as well were substantial. Khrushchev reacted by intensifying his demand for corn acreage and in 1956 a further increase was called for. Because of a dry summer in the European part of the Soviet Union, 1956 was also a good year for corn, and thus the program of corn expansion was viewed as a major victory in agriculture. Everyone jumped on the corn bandwagon. New silos were planned, systems of feeding livestock with corn silage

[*] *Narodnoe khoziaistvo SSSR v 1958g* (The National Economy of the Soviet Union in 1958) (Moscow: Central Statistical Administration [TsSU], 1959), p. 403.

were worked out, special equipment to mechanize planting was made available, and the production of pure strains of corn was improved. A special corn research institute was established in the Ukraine; at the Agricultural Exhibit in Moscow a Corn Pavilion was opened. The Ministry of Agriculture offered a new scientific journal entitled *Corn;* the Ministry of Food Production increased the number of food products made from corn and opened a special store in Moscow called "Corn." Corn, like the virgin lands, became a symbol of a new world in agriculture—an agricultural miracle.

chapter seven

KHRUSHCHEV ASCENDANT

☼

WE now come to a most important event of Khrushchev's years in power, his so-called "secret" speech at the Twentieth Party Congress in February 1956 in which he denounced government-by-fear and Stalinist terror (and, by implication, Stalin himself). Thus he took an irretrievable step toward committing himself to the creation of a new climate in the Soviet Union and in the Communist movement as a whole.

THE "SECRET" SPEECH

There is no hard evidence that, after Beria's arrest and the circulation of a confidential letter among central and local Party activists listing detailed accusations against him, Khrushchev already intended to link Beria's guilt with Stalin and to denounce Stalin's crimes as well, that is, to do exactly what he did at the Twentieth Congress. At the end of 1953, Stalin was not yet an official target for criticism. But when the Stalin Prizes were not awarded on his birthday, December 21 (since 1939 an uninterrupted tradition for outstanding achievement in science, technology, and the arts), it was obvious that the official explanation offered—reasons of economy—in no way reflected the true state of affairs.

Neither Khrushchev nor his colleagues on the Central Committee had any real idea of the true extent of repression, but all of them recognized the need to face the question. It was clearly impossible to continue the rehabilitation of political prisoners without a thorough examination of Stalin's role. To this end, the Central Committee established a special commission to prepare a report with recommendations.

Although its ostensible mandate was to investigate all aspects of Stalinist terror, the commission was not expected to present the total picture in the full light of day—rather it was to give a partial view with special lighting effects. The report was to condemn the abuses of power that had temporarily engulfed healthy elements in the Party, but at the same time it was to defend as inevitable and necessary the measures taken against "internal and external enemies of Lenin's party" at a time when the new socialist system was in the process of creation. The Kremlin elite convinced themselves that Stalin was justified in liquidating Trotsky's "left" opposition as well as the "left" and "right" deviations that surfaced at the end of the 1920s. The ruthless collectivization of farms and peasantry and the drastic treatment of the kulaks were excluded from censure as being necessary. Such measures were deemed to be manifestations of the class struggle inevitable in any socialist revolution. What was intolerable were the repressions taken against dedicated Party workers, independent-minded scientists, artists, writers, and musicians, and thousands of ordinary people inadvertently caught in the net—this was another matter altogether.

The cautious approach of the leadership determined the composition of the commission; those named to it were known as "moderates" and P. N. Pospelov, basically a typical Stalinist and once chairman of a commission to write a biography of Stalin, was appointed to head it. An extremely conservative Party historian, a participant in many acts of mass repression in the 1930s who used lofty theoretical arguments to justify immediate practical ends, Pospelov was as unsuited to supervise an exposé of terror as he had been to compose a biography of Stalin.

The commission's report was prepared for the exclusive use of the Presidium of the Central Committee. Even Pospelov was unable to conceal how Stalin willfully and illegally settled accounts with Party leaders who incurred his disfavor—former members of the Stalin Politburo, members of plenums of the Central Committee, delegates to Party Congresses, secretaries of oblast and city Party committees, and officials of the Executive Committee of the Comintern—because the members of the Central Committee were already aware of these actions. Indeed, they themselves had lived under the threat of similar treatment.

Even in its highly selective approach, the 1955 Pospelov report had a staggering effect, revealing as it did Stalin's obsessive destruction of loyal Party and government workers and Army middle and top officers. Although, in 1955, members of the Presidium knew part of the story, nobody had an accurate picture of the extent of his repressive policy throughout the nation. The information provided by Pospelov's commission made a profound impression and the Presidium resolved to criticize abuses of power during "the personality cult era" at the Twentieth Party Congress scheduled for February 1956. This general unfocused criticism was included in the official minutes of the Central Committee and was written into speeches scheduled for delivery by members of the Party Presidium at the Congress. In this way the Party leaders would demonstrate the steadfast intent of the new leadership to return to the methods of socialist legality. However the official agenda did not include any speech by Khrushchev specifically devoted to Stalin's crimes, and no such speech had been formally endorsed by either the Presidium or the Plenum of the Central Committee.

The Congress met, heard the scheduled speeches, and formally concluded with the election of new members to the Central Committee Plenum and with the election of Khrushchev as First Secretary of the Party's Central Committee. By tradition the nomination of the Presidium of the Central Committee and the assignment of administrative responsibilities for its members then becomes the prerogative of the First Secretary as part of his proposals to the newly elected Plenum. During this brief interval between the election of the Plenum and the nomination of the Presidium, Khrushchev, seizing the opportunity of the short period of unchecked power he had,* made his dramatic move. He called for an extension of the already officially adjourned Congress (many delegates had already left and had to return from their hotels).

The call for delegates to return to Kremlin Hall for a "closed" Congress meeting came about half an hour before midnight of February 24. No one from the foreign delegations was invited, neither from the socialist countries of Eastern Europe, nor from the Chinese People's Republic, nor from noncommunist countries. The Congress was chaired by Khrushchev himself and about midnight he began what was to be a four-hour speech. In a frank but emotional manner he spoke of terrible things—of the imprisonment of thousands of blameless people, of the torture and execution of devoted and innocent Party leaders, of unjustifiable deportations, of Stalin's personal directives calling for terror, torture, and death, of grave costly mistakes made during the war, and other instances of malfeasance of office.

The speech was not followed by general discussion or debate, nor was any special resolution adopted. The general psychologi-

---

* During this interval (at most overnight), the First Secretary works alone because there is no Presidium for him to be answerable to.

cal impact was overwhelming and the stunned delegates listened in silence, then left the Kremlin and returned home.

The "secret" nature of Khrushchev's speech was, of course, mere pretense. Within days, the Secretariat of the Central Committee issued a directive that the text be read to groups of Party activists throughout the nation; then it was read at "closed" general Party meetings in all factories, institutions, businesses, and other organizations; several days after that it was read to those outside the Party, at meetings of industrial and office workers, kolkhozniks, university students, and even to senior students in secondary schools. The speech thus became known throughout the Soviet Union. Copies were dispatched to all Communist Party leaders, both in socialist and capitalist countries, and it was soon published abroad in almost all languages, including Russian. However, it never has been published within the Soviet Union.*

The Aftermath

Within the Soviet Union, the speech was hailed by most of the intelligentsia and Khrushchev became enormously popular, although in certain areas denunciations of Stalin were unwelcome. In Georgia (where Stalin was born), for instance, anti-Khrushchev disturbances broke out as a reaction against any denigration of the "Great Son of the Georgian people."

There was also opposition in other socialist countries, in Poland, Rumania, Bulgaria, Hungary, Czechoslovakia, East Germany, Albania, and China. Khrushchev's speech had come as a shocking surprise for the leaders of these countries. He had failed to consider the hard truth that many of these men had been disciples of Stalin and Beria and that, in the process of nurturing "personality cults" of their own, they had employed

---

* One million copies of the booklet with Khrushchev's speech were printed for open sale. After a more moderate resolution in June 1956, the whole printing was destroyed. A few copies survived, and the authors saw one such booklet.

similar techniques of repression; but in such cases it was not a question of terror back in the remote years of 1937–38, but of terror in a recent close-at-hand period—1948–52. The Party leadership in these countries strongly pressured the Soviet Communist Party to renounce de-Stalinization.

At home, within the Presidium of the Central Committee itself, Malenkov, Kaganovich, Voroshilov, and Molotov openly opposed the new course of de-Stalinization. In his speech Khrushchev had limited his accusations chiefly to charges against Stalin, Yezhov, Beria, and a few others, and there was even the unofficial opinion that certain leaders, such as Khrushchev, Molotov, Kaganovich, Voroshilov, and Malenkov, not only had not taken a direct part in the repressions but had actually restrained Stalin as far as they could.

The overall emotional reaction to Khrushchev's speech was so intense that he had to put a temporary check on de-Stalinization measures (an off-again on-again policy that was to characterize the next several years) and allow the adoption in June 1956 of a resolution ("Overcoming of the Cult of Personality and Its Consequences") that gave credit to Stalin's services to the Party, the nation, and the international revolutionary movement and that characterized his crimes merely as misguided abuses of power. In addition the scale of these abuses was toned down, and the assertion was made that the basic "Leninist core" of the Central Committee had persevered even under Stalin and had exerted a restraining influence on his actions, even though it had been unable to remove him from power.

However, this moderate resolution could no longer halt the course of events set in motion by Khrushchev's revelations. Riots in Poland in the autumn of 1956 were directly related to the discrediting of former Polish Party leaders and brought about a radical shake-up of the Polish Central Committee and the rise of Gomulka to power. Events were even more dramatic in Hungary, where the bloody terror of Rákosi, a disciple of Stalin and Beria, was still fresh in people's memories. The dictatorship of the Hungarian Party rapidly collapsed and, after a long period of indecision, Khrushchev ordered Soviet troops to march against the Hungarian insurgents.

Before making this move, he sought the opinions of Party leaders in China and in each of the Warsaw Pact countries. All sanctioned use of military force, including the Poles. Mao Tse-tung, while acknowledging the necessity of military intervention, reproached Khrushchev for seeking China's advice too late—the time for consultation was before Khrushchev decided to "becloud the name of the great leader of the international workers' movement, the true Marxist-Leninist, Comrade Stalin."

In this letter, the Chinese were openly giving notice that Khrushchev could no longer be accepted as the leader of international Communism; he had betrayed the ideals of Marxism-Leninism and become a revisionist, and the leading role in the world Communist movement would now belong to the Chinese Communist Party, on whose banners the portrait of Stalin remained in between those of Lenin and Mao. On Party posters Mao had gradually become the fifth classic figure of Marxism (after Marx, Engels, Lenin, and Stalin), but now his portrait was drawn noticeably larger than the others—a pleasure which he had not permitted himself during Stalin's lifetime or prior to Khrushchev's denunciation of Stalin at the Twentieth Party Congress.

Perhaps more significant and far-reaching than the political reactions to Khrushchev's speech were the theoretical, philosophical, and psychological ones. The denunciation of Stalinism at the Twentieth Party Congress and the mass rehabilitation of political prisoners, while transforming Khrushchev into a hero, nevertheless threw a serious doubt on Communist ideology as a whole. It was now apparent to the whole world that the Soviet system of government, born of a revolution, had been unable to guarantee fundamental democratic freedoms and legal rights to its citizens, had been unable to develop and maintain itself on a basis of *law* and constitution, and had relied on terror to strangle any opposition. There had been hopes that after the Twentieth Congress, these evils would soon become obsolete, but the events of 1956—the suppression of the Hungarian rebellion by force, the renewed deterioration of relations with Yugoslavia because of the Hungarian tragedy—indicated a departure from the firm resolve of the Twentieth Congress; de-Stalinization and democratization had been diverted under pressure both at home and from Communist Party leaders abroad.

For literary circles, the clearest sign of "liberalization" had been the publication of Dudintsev's novel *Not by Bread Alone,* which caused a welcome sensation among intellectuals. This novel sharply criticized bureaucracy and showed how the disposition of bureaucratic whim under Stalin had spawned a pseudo-elite which had hindered the nation's technological progress. Even the timid moves toward scientific and technical cooperation with other countries revealed stagnation in many fields. For example, the Soviet Union at the time lacked the simplest type of computer technology and had no synthetic fiber industry. But the springtime was soon over. At the end of 1956 Khrushchev personally labeled Dudintsev's novel "anti-Soviet." The "thaw" (the term is Ilya Ehrenburg's) in literature was coming to an end. It was at this time that Pasternak's novel *Doctor Zhivago* was rejected for publication in the Soviet Union, but this did not become known until 1958, when Pasternak was awarded the Nobel Prize.

Khrushchev's speeches now took on a more conservative tone as he attempted to partially exonerate Stalin as a Party and government leader. Similarly there was an undeclared moratorium on any further probes into the past or on additional denunciations of bygone crimes or their perpetrators. The reign of terror and caprice had by no means begun with the murder of Kirov in 1934, nor had it been limited only to those Party leaders who were now rehabilitated (at the Twentieth Party Congress Khrushchev had stated that some 7,000 Party workers were being rehabilitated, but within a few months after the Congress, from 8 to 9 million were rehabilitated). The moratorium precluded any consideration of rehabilitating those active opposers of Stalin who had been convicted at "open" trials (Bukharin, Zinoviev, Kamenev, Rykov, etc.) as well as any overall review of the Party's entire policy since the October Revolution. Under such circumstances, a review of the repressions in the collectivization period would be unavoidable as would a review of the 1929–30 trials and much more besides, including the Leon Trotsky question. Khrushchev and his colleagues were reluctant to undermine the foundations of their own power, power which had been gained under the old system.

These limitations on rehabilitation made an unfavorable impression on world opinion, particularly within leftist movements. In the Soviet Union, disenchantment was rooted more in the abysmally low standard of living that prevailed than in political considerations. People would be convinced of the superiority of the Soviet system only if it could be shown that all the sacrifices demanded by centralization and dictatorial methods produced tangible economic results—not in the form of heavy industry but in the availability of consumer goods, foodstuffs, and clothing as well as improved housing and working conditions.

It was Khrushchev who above all was given credit for alleviating the rigors of kolkhoz life, for lifting the shadow of police terror, for sending at least a trickle of consumer goods to the general populace; the initial success of the virgin lands and corn programs brought him prestige, and he was thought to be the one responsible for the general air of euphoria that could be felt throughout the country. Although others had assisted in opening the Pandora's box of Stalin's misdeeds, it was Khrushchev who had stood up and made the speech before the Twentieth Congress and who was now basking in the limelight as a result.

THE DRAMATIC EVENTS OF 1957

In pursuit of his dream to shower the country with consumer goods, Khrushchev, while speaking at a Leningrad meeting in May 1957, put forth a scheme for a spectacular leap forward in the production of meat, milk, and butter. He exhorted the nation to overtake U.S. production in three to four years (i.e., by 1960–61). The Presidium of the Central Committee had not been consulted about this goal. Khrushchev was simply a victim of his own exuberance and of his overestimation of what the influence of the Party leader could realistically be on the agricultural sectors of the economy. This became clear from his Leningrad speech.

Overtaking the United States in milk and butter production was quite possible, since U.S. consumption of milk and butter had already declined as a result of an increase in vegetable oil and margarine production. In fact in 1957 U.S. and Soviet butter production were almost equal (U.S. consumption of butter was two to three times lower than that in European countries). In meat production, however, the Soviet Union lagged far behind the United States, and Khrushchev's call to eliminate the gap in three to four years was unrealistic.

In 1957 the Soviet Union produced 7.5 million tons of meat, or 36 kilograms per capita; the United States produced over 16 million tons—97 kilograms per capita.* Thus the Soviet Union's meat output would have to triple in three years. Khrushchev was relying primarily on greater feed resources, especially corn. As if realizing the improbability of his whole scheme, he generously made the deadline flexible:

> It won't be any tragedy if, for instance, in 1960 we still can't surpass America in meat production. We can allow an extension—

* *Narodnoe khoziaistvo SSSR v 1958g* (The National Economy of the Soviet Union in 1958) (Moscow: Central Statistical Administration [TsSU], 1959), p. 469.

there's no harm in not solving this problem until 1961. But in 1961 we should be "mopping up," as they say, and have the basic groundwork laid by 1960. We've got to get busy right now and lick this problem.

As we now know, it was this speech—as much news to the Central Committee as it was to Khrushchev's audience in Leningrad—that was the immediate impetus for the formation of an opposition group determined to unseat Khrushchev as First Secretary. He was viewed as an irresponsible adventurist. The nucleus of the group included his steadfast critics—Molotov, Malenkov, and Kaganovich—who knew full well that Khrushchev's ascendancy was at their own expense. Voroshilov joined the conspiracy out of fear, and even Bulganin acquiesced. The plan to remove Khrushchev was set while he and Bulganin were on a trip to Finland. There were official welcoming ceremonies upon his return to Moscow, and pictures of Presidium members warmly greeting Khrushchev appeared in the newspapers. The next day, however, Khrushchev had to face a meeting of the Presidium of the Central Committee.

The meeting of the Presidium lasted some three days, and during this time none of its members left Presidium headquarters in the Kremlin. After heated debate, not recorded in the official minutes, Khrushchev was dismissed as First Secretary by a vote of 8 to 4; his only supporters were Suslov, Furtseva, and Mikoyan (the fourth vote was his own). However, Khrushchev refused to accept the decision, insisting that a full plenum of the Central Committee be called. This was a legitimate demand since, according to Party statutes, the First Secretary is elected and/or removed by the Plenum of the Central Committee, not its Presidium. Well aware of this, the opposition bloc had taken all possible precautions to avoid the convening of a full plenum and intended to arrest Khrushchev if he refused to submit to Presidium orders.

However, word of the long secret meeting and its true pur-

pose leaked out. If all resolutions adopted could have been im-
plemented on the very first day, the anti-Khrushchev conspiracy
might have succeeded but, by the second day, more than
twenty members of the Central Committee had sensed something was occurring and arrived at the Kremlin, demanding admission to the meeting. It so happened that Kremlin security
was in the hands of a man loyal to Khrushchev, A. Serov. Nor
could the opposition call in the Army, because the Army was
headed by Marshal Zhukov, who had been restored to power
and prestige by Khrushchev.

At this time, Leningrad was observing the 250th anniversary
of its founding, and many oblast secretaries were attending the
celebration. Frol Kozlov, secretary of the Leningrad oblast committee, was a Khrushchev supporter. As soon as he learned
what was going on in Moscow, he went there immediately, accompanied by even more members of the Central Committee.
After they were refused admittance, they formed a task force
headed by Zhukov, Kozlov, and Serov. To strengthen their
ranks by bringing other Central Committee members to Moscow, Zhukov ordered the use of military jets. By June 21, more
than 100 members were assembled in the Kremlin and it was
no longer possible to avoid convening a Central Committee plenum to discuss "the Khrushchev question." *

The Plenum opened on June 22. Its session lasted more than
thirty hours with almost no recess. Again, the debate was not
recorded. According to official reports, the Plenum listened to
speeches by Khrushchev on "The Internal Situation in the
Communist Party of the Soviet Union" and by Molotov on "The
International Position of the Soviet Union." But the real issue
being decided was the fate of Khrushchev, who won the support
of an overwhelming majority of the Plenum. In many cases the

---

* There were in all some 300 members of the Central Committee, and according
to Party rules a vote by one-third is sufficient to convene an extraordinary plenum.

Party leaders of regions and national republics were already protégés of Khrushchev, who felt that under Khrushchev they had
received more power and autonomy. No one wanted a restoration of the Malenkov-Molotov-Kaganovich troika and the young
Party elite opposed the possibility of a return to the old methods
of terror. The Plenum completely reorganized the Presidium,
and dismissed the three chief conspirators (plus Shepilov, who
had joined the plot) not only from Presidium membership but
also from the Central Committee. For tactical considerations,
the four other Presidium members who had voted against
Khrushchev were not dismissed from the Central Committee although they were strongly reprimanded. The sudden removal of
eight Presidium members at once might have given the impression that a crisis was in the offing or that a coup was under
way. In the future, the maneuvers of the conspirators were to
be referred to as the "Anti-Party Plot."

A new Presidium was elected, with membership expanded
from eleven to fifteen. Khrushchev supporters were rewarded—
Zhukov, Frol Kozlov, and some others became members of the
new Presidium.

The four leaders of the Anti-Party group were not given the
grim punishments that would have been their lot in the old
days. They were not sent to prison camps or secretly executed.
Molotov, who had scowled through diplomatic conferences
around the world, was made the ambassador to Mongolia;
Malenkov, once in charge of the whole of Soviet industry, was
appointed the director of a power station in a remote corner
of Central Asia; and Kaganovich, who had once been boss of the
Ukraine, was made director of a cement factory in Sverdlovsk.
Shepilov, an economist, became a professor in one of the Moscow colleges. By these relatively mild reprisals, the new leadership of the Central Committee showed that terror was no longer
needed to run the country or the Party.

With other opponents now quietly submissive, Khrushchev

became the sole and undisputed leader of the Party and of the Soviet Union.

While Zhukov was on an official visit to Yugoslavia in October 1957, Khrushchev unexpectedly dismissed him as minister of defense. The decision was made before Zhukov's return but was not published until afterward, so that Zhukov's first inkling that something was amiss came when there were no official greeting ceremonies at the airport. He had not been charged with any misconduct; it was simply that his prestige in the Army had grown too great, and Khrushchev feared the possibility of a military coup. The simple official explanation was that Zhukov was guilty of "Bonapartism."

In October 1957, a triumph of a completely different kind awaited Khrushchev—the successful launching of the first artificial earth satellite. This dramatic event had stunning impact and enhanced the international prestige of the Soviet Union. In a highly impressive way the Soviet Union demonstrated its superiority over the United States in a crucial sphere of technology. It was the first Soviet victory in Khrushchev's newly proclaimed contest of "peaceful competition" with the United States.

Indirectly it was also a personal political victory for Khrushchev and not only because he had given a particularly high priority to missile technology. The chief designer of Soviet rockets was Sergei Pavlovich Korolev, without whom neither the first sputnik nor Yuri Gagarin's first space flight would have been possible. Korolev's research group of rocketry specialists had been formed in prison back in Stalin's day. Korolev had been arrested before the war and had been sent to the frightful Kolyma gold-mining camps. He was arrested *because* of his work in rocket technology—being accused of neglecting and thus sabotaging work on standard aircraft. The potential of rocketry was recognized only toward the end of the war, when the German V-2s had demonstrated their effectiveness. Korolev was allowed to organize a design group within the MGB system—but he worked in it at first as a prisoner. The reorganization of state security after Beria's execution and the abolition of such prison-scientific centers made it possible to release Korolev and appoint him chief designer of the Soviet space program.

Thus at the end of 1957, Khrushchev became the undisputed and vastly popular leader of his country. He had the enthusiastic support of all segments of Soviet society and the program for the future was clear—the Soviet Union would travel the highway of quick development of agriculture, consumer-goods production, internal democratization, and improved relations with other countries to relax international tensions. Every small sign of this happier plan was important. For example, ever since Stalin's time all new housing in Moscow and other cities had, by law, to be built with underground bomb shelters. After 1957 these expensive shelters were no longer required as an integral part of the housing program, a clear sign of confidence that the country was on its way to peace and prosperity.

chapter eight

KHRUSHCHEV OVERRIDING

AFTER Stalin's aloof and unapproachable manner, his living and working behind heavily guarded Kremlin walls, most people liked Khrushchev's easy style and actually enjoyed his peripatetic jaunts around the country, his attention-getting trips abroad—and even his incessant speeches. Khrushchev literally opened the Kremlin gates to the people for the first time since 1930. Ordinary citizens were allowed to enter the area freely and see the famous churches and other treasures. Only certain government buildings were closed to the public.

Khrushchev's anti-Stalinism was especially attractive to the Soviet intelligentsia and the brighter political atmosphere made him very popular, not only among the intelligentsia but also among industrial workers and peasants, for whom economic improvements took first place. A higher standard of living for the average person, the expansion of housing construction, the emergence of the USSR from the dark ages of international isolation—all these changes for the better were quite properly attributed to Khrushchev's extroverted leadership.

The entire world press was Khrushchev-conscious, and every day his name appeared with insistent repetition in major newspapers. His power was virtually unlimited. After Bulganin's exit from the political arena in 1958, Khrushchev, now Chairman of the Council of Ministers as well as First Secretary, became in effect a dictator, enjoying total power not by employing the methods of terror but rather by appointing to key posts in the Party structure, the Council of Ministers, and the Army, people whose careers he personally had advanced at one time or another. These were men and women whom he trusted and whom he had known either in his prewar days, or during the war and the postwar years. The Procurator-General, the Chairman of the KGB, the Minister of Defense, the Chairman of the Presidium of the Supreme Soviet, the majority of the secretaries of the Central Committee, and many oblast committee secretaries constituted Khrushchev's personal "party" within the nation's leadership and he could always be sure of their loyalty and support.

In these circumstances, Khrushchev was able to make a great number of new, often unanticipated changes without encountering opposition of any consequence. Stalin had been able to make mistakes, to miscalculate, and to carry out his nefarious schemes without loss of power, because the "cult of personality" rendered impotent any sort of conspiracy against him (although he was in constant fear of such conspiracies). By 1959–60, a "personality cult" has also arisen around Khrushchev, and he too could make errors and miscalculate without any serious qualms about loss of power. Khrushchev-watchers could only wonder what he would do next. Clothed in infallibility, he could do no wrong in the eyes of the majority of Soviet citizens.

He had his critics, but initially they were only those who opposed him for the wrong reasons. Grim bureaucrats trained under Stalin, a discontented segment of the military high command, displaced technocrats from now-defunct industrial ministries (abolished by Khrushchev's "decentralization" reform)—all these were unfavorably disposed toward him. The last-mentioned felt especially resentful.

After the closure of many specialized industrial ministries in 1957, thousands of governmental functionaries were transferred from Moscow to jobs on regional economic councils in "sovnarkhoz" regional centers throughout the USSR. Having to leave Moscow or even a capital of a republic was an extremely unwelcome change. It was difficult to exchange the sophisticated level of culture and higher standard of living found in the capitals for the simpler pleasures of provincial (mostly industrial) cities.

Khrushchev also abolished the sizable monthly salary "bonus" given to senior officials (secretaries of oblast committees, members of central committees, and editors-in-chief of newspapers, etc.), thus reducing their incomes, despite increases in their regular salaries. Other senior officials (directors of institutes, heads of ministry departments, assistant directors of factories, and so on) found that perquisites such as official cars with chauffeurs for trips of any sort were no longer available. These changes were not very popular with those who had benefited in the past, but were greeted with approval by the intelligentsia and by the general public as well. Such measures were seen as attempts to bring the leaders closer to the people and as a step toward democracy, reducing the disparities in living standards between public officials and ordinary citizens and making the pyramid of power a more gently sloping structure.

At about this time Khrushchev, in typical thunderbolt fashion, rather weakly bolstered by a somewhat vague excuse, unexpectedly called for the immediate return of the many thousands of Soviet specialists and technical advisers working in China, where they had been sent under terms of an agreement on technical cooperation (the excuse being that they were badly treated, oversubjected to surveillance, and unheeded when offering advice or expertise). The abrupt departure of this highly skilled group disrupted the Chinese economy and made the quarrel with the Chinese leaders irreversible. Repercussions reached as far as Czechoslovakia, as China was immediately obliged to cancel a number of large orders it had placed with Czech factories. But the falling-out with China, which could have been avoided by proceeding more temperately, was credited by the Soviet press as a political achievement.

Later an astonished world watched him pound a UN lectern with his shoe during a speech delivered by the Spanish delegate, but this outburst was described in *Izvestia* (whose editor, A. Adzhubei, was his son-in-law) as an heroic feat. He unjustly accused UN Secretary-General Dag Hammarskjöld of abetting a conspiracy against Patrice Lumumba, the pro-Soviet leader of the Congo. When Lumumba was murdered, Khrushchev announced that the Soviet Union would refuse to recognize Hammarskjöld as Secretary-General or to have any dealings with him. Not only was this a violation of the UN charter, it was inconsistent, since Hammarskjöld's candidacy for the post had been strongly supported by the Soviet Union. Only Hammarskjöld's tragic and untimely death in a plane crash in the Congo forestalled the UN crisis that was about to erupt as a result of Khrushchev's about face. Again, his sudden shift was praised in the Soviet Union.

Khrushchev twice fomented a "Berlin crisis," the second one ending with the construction of the Berlin Wall—but even this did not undermine his domestic or international prestige. He received full approval as the peacemaker for the Cuban missile confrontation in 1962, even though he had actually capitulated to President Kennedy.

Not only in foreign affairs, but also at home, Khrushchev practically had carte blanche to act in whatever way he chose. He was of course sustained by the aura of infallibility that still clung to orders emanating from the First Secretary of the Central Committee/Chairman of the Council of Ministers. In addition, the rapid and constant rotation and reappointments of senior officials prevented the formation of an opposition bloc. The speed with which Khrushchev carried out his programs allowed no one time to forecast or evaluate possible results. Furthermore, almost any plan proposed by the leader of the Party was assured of broad public support in "nationwide discussions." Even the scheduled plenums of the Central Committee, which had an important decision-making function in 1953–57, were transformed into enormous rallies held in the Kremlin Palace of Congresses. Thousands of prominent people, Party workers and former activists, were invited to attend; this could hardly facilitate the raising of serious objections.

With such popularity and political acumen, how and why was Khrushchev ousted?

In the Western press, Khrushchev's "fall" was often portrayed as the result of a traditional "struggle for power"—much like those that removed Beria, Malenkov, Bulganin, or others. This was an incomplete, inexact, and incorrect version of events. Such an interpretation coincided with Khrushchev's own point of view. Until the end of his life he was incapable of recognizing that his own misjudgments had driven him from office. At last there came a time when every action was no longer uncritically accepted as a "great achievement"—it even became possible to apply the term "mistake."

BACKFIRE FROM THE MACHINE-TRACTOR STATIONS

One of the most radical of Khrushchev's agricultural reforms, begun and completed virtually within a single year, was one of his most serious errors in judgment—the abolition of the state-controlled machine-tractor stations and the transfer of all their agricultural equipment to the kolkhozes. This reorganization seemed, on paper, a logical step after the amalgamation of kolkhozes undertaken in 1950.

When collectivization began, it had not been feasible for the small kolkhozes to purchase and operate efficiently all the necessary agricultural machinery needed on a farm. Nor did the government wish to put this equipment and therefore the entire means of agricultural production under kolkhoz control alone, which is why it had originally created different types of agricultural units: sovkhozes, kolkhozes, and machine-tractor stations (MTS).

After the consolidation of the kolkhozes in 1950, one machine-tractor station might be servicing a single large kolkhoz, although in the majority of cases each station still serviced several farms. In those instances where one station serviced one kolkhoz, it seemed natural to merge the two under one administration. In 1957 in the Stavropol region, where large kolkhozes have several thousands of hectares of land each, such a merger was tried on an experimental basis for twelve machine-tractor stations servicing twelve large kolkhozes. Under the terms of the merger, the chairman of the kolkhoz was also appointed the director of the station serving the kolkhoz. Results of the experiment showed that the utilization of equipment became more efficient, the quality of agricultural labor improved, and management was simplified in that there was no longer a need for liaison between kolkhoz and machine-tractor station at the raion level.

Although the Stavropol experience demonstrated the feasibility of merger, many ramifications of the project had yet to be considered. Further experimentation should have been carried out involving other variables, for example, a situation where one machine-tractor station serviced not a single large kolkhoz, but rather several large or medium-sized ones.* Where the ma-

* The phrase "large kolkhoz" does not imply a standard indication of size and is interpreted differently in different localities. The area of a "large kolkhoz" can vary from 20,000 hectares down to 500 or 600 hectares, depending on whether it is in Kazakhstan, in the Stavropol region (south), in the Ukraine, or in the Moscow or Leningrad regions (north). In the eastern or southern parts of the

chine-tractor station served a single large kolkhoz, it was simple to merge the two without any complicated reorganization of equipment, repair shops, or workers' housing arrangements, etc. But such cases were the exception.

Inspired by the results in Stavropol, Khrushchev expressed a number of random thoughts on the feasibility of merger. These were preliminary ideas and needed careful thought and testing. But Khrushchev was too impatient to wait. A few months later, at his urging the Central Committee issued a directive ordering machine-tractor stations to transfer their equipment to the kolkhozes.

Earlier, Khrushchev had spoken of the necessity for a *gradual* and selective reorganization of the machine-tractor stations; it would not be universal and would take place only in those districts where the kolkhozes were capable of using the equipment properly, and where each station serviced only one or two, or possibly three, kolkhozes. In the central, western, and northern zones, where kolkhozes were smaller and less efficient, the process of transformation was not to begin for several years, or even later.*

But in March 1958 Khrushchev promptly disregarded his own counsels of moderation and in practice, backed by a directive from the Central Committee, forced the acceleration of the program. Three months after reorganization began, a majority of the machine-tractor stations were abolished. And, although not a part of the original plan, instead of *mergers* between the kolkhozes and machine-tractor stations, the kolkhozes were required to *purchase* MTS equipment from the government. It had taken the government decades to amass and pay for this equipment, and now it was expected that the kolkhozes could

country the farms were usually much larger than in the central and northern areas.

* N. S. Khrushchev, *Stroitel'stvo Kommunizma v SSSR* (The Building of Communism in the Soviet Union) (Moscow, 1964), 3:131–32.

buy that same equipment in a single year. By the end of 1958, more than 80 percent of all kolkhozes had been forced to purchase MTS equipment and no longer made use of MTS services—this figure included both poor and better-off kolkhozes. Some 20 percent, the extremely poor kolkhozes, already deep in debt, could not afford to purchase any machinery at all, but the Central Committee decreed that these kolkhozes must buy as well, although on credit to prevent them from developing "an attitude of dependency." Thus by January 1959 practically all machine-tractor stations had been absorbed: of 8,000 stations, only 345 remained, and by the end of 1959 there were only 34.* Thus Khrushchev's sensible estimate of a time span of several years had been foolishly reduced to less than twelve months.

This kind of crash program, which conflicted with a decree (law) adopted by the Supreme Soviet and ignored all individual peculiarities, inflicted great economic and organizational damage. In theory, the total value on paper of all MTS equipment, based on the prices paid when the machinery came from the factories, was supposed to be only 17 percent of what the state paid into the kolkhozes for their produce. Thus it was assumed that the kolkhozes could afford this compulsory purchase of equipment without going bankrupt.

In reality, the situation was much more complex. Aside from the cost of the equipment itself, the kolkhozes had to lay out sizable amounts to construct buildings to house the new machinery, to install fuel storage facilities, and to build repair shops. Furthermore kolkhozes now had to pay the wages of machine operators, who had previously been paid by the government.

The legal regulations covering the sale of MTS equipment had provided for installment payments over three to five years.

* *Narodnoe khoziaistvo SSSR v 1961g* (The National Economy of the Soviet Union in 1961) (Moscow: Central Statistical Administration [TsSU], 1962), p. 291.

But early on in the program, a group of affluent kolkhozes announced a "drive" to pay for the equipment within a year. Khrushchev lauded their "initiative" and under this oblique pressure nearly all the kolkhozes paid up in that time. To do so, many kolkhozes had to cancel plans for other projects, halt construction already begun, postpone the purchase of facilities for cattle raising, or appropriate funds set aside for wages. Sometimes part of the working capital to meet food production costs was diverted to this purpose.*

The sale of MTS equipment itself was very badly organized. Naturally the kolkhozes first took the newer machinery which had not yet been heavily used. No one wanted to buy the older tractors or trucks, particularly since the prices were the same for both new and worn items. It would have been logical for heavily used machinery to have been priced at a lower rate or even given away, but the government did not permit itself such generosity; the kolkhozes were pressured into buying all of the old machinery as well as the new, at the identical price.

In addition, all the preliminary calculations of the value placed on MTS equipment, which had been compared to kolkhoz "incomes" in Khrushchev's initial proposals, were far from accurate. In the past the state had produced the equipment and delivered it to the MTS at a given price, perhaps one that corresponded to the factory's production costs or perhaps even one assigned at random. When this same equipment was resold to the kolkhozes, a new *wholesale* price was set, which on the average was twice the previous one. Thus the kolkhozes were forced to purchase the equipment not at the government's original price, but at an arbitrary new commercial one. Not surprisingly, the prices of gasoline, lubricants, and spare parts were more than doubled at the same time.

If the liquidation of machine-tractor stations was to be judged

* *Voprosy ekonomiki* (Problems of Economics), 1965, no. 6, p. 5.

by the speed with which it was carried out, the program could easily be considered a successful one. However, if it was a question of improving agricultural conditions, the evaluation would be rather different. The negative effects of the program became apparent as early as 1959–60, and could certainly have been anticipated and avoided if more thought could have been devoted to the whole plan. Agriculture sustained a long-term injury which has not been completely healed to the present day. The worst consequences of the machine-tractor "reform" were the following:

1. The kolkhozes had to spend so much money on equipment that many important and essential projects in the planning stage had to be abandoned or deferred, especially plans for constructing new dairy facilities or for modernizing animal husbandry.

2. There were not enough properly trained technicians on the kolkhozes to operate the agricultural machinery with any efficiency. Rural agriculture lost about 50 percent of the drivers and operators who had previously worked in the MTS system. Not surprisingly, very few MTS workers wanted to join the kolkhozes under the new plan. Instead, the more highly skilled sought employment in the cities and industrial towns, often commuting from their home villages or former MTS settlements.

The reason was the world of difference in status between an MTS worker (i.e., a government employee) and a kolkhoznik— and more was involved than wages alone. The kolkhozes might have been able to meet MTS wage levels, but they were in no position to guarantee the legal and social privileges enjoyed at the stations. An MTS tractor driver was a *blue-collar worker* and, as such, had an internal passport enabling him to move and to seek employment wherever he wanted within the Soviet Union; he had seniority and was entitled to a state pension, a government-paid vacation, and many other trade union workers' rights that a kolkhoznik, virtually tied to one place, did not yet enjoy in 1958.

To plug this drain on skilled labor, the government offered half-measures to make kolkhoz life more attractive—pensions and vacations for kolkhozniks, as well as the possibility for MTS operators to be hired by a kolkhoz without having to become a member, etc. But even these measures were offered too late, after too many workers had already left for other employment.

3. With no time to build facilities to house the new machinery while losing many of those trained to take care of it, the kolkhozes in 1959–61 lost substantial amounts of equipment that fell into disrepair or wore out prematurely.

4. An unforeseen but devastating negative result of the program was a sudden crisis in the Soviet Union's massive agricultural equipment industry. Up to 1958, factories producing tractors and combines, etc., turned out their quotas according to plan and shipped their input to the machine-tractor stations as directed. But after 1959, the machine-tractor stations no longer existed, and now the kolkhozes were expected to do all the purchasing. The kolkhozes, however, had exhausted all their available funds in buying used equipment from the stations. Besides they had no qualified buyers, people trained to evaluate and buy directly from the factory. Sales dropped sharply. To avoid a slowdown in production, equipment was shipped to the virgin lands or exported but, nevertheless, the *manufacture* of agricultural machinery declined alarmingly as enormous accumulations of unsold machinery began to pile up at the factories (see table).

Even by 1971 the delivery of combines to agriculture was two times below the 1957 level. Production of silage combines decreased by a factor of four in 1957–60. There were fewer orders for tractor-mounted plows, sowers, cultivators, mowers, and binders. The delivery of some types of equipment virtually halted. Examples could go on and on. Indices of utilization of

	PURCHASED BY MTS, 1957	PURCHASED BY KOLKHOZES, 1959/60
Agricultural tractors	258,000	236,000
Combines (wheat, rye, etc.)	134,000	53,000
Pick-up trucks	125,000	66,000
Grain dryers	13,000	900
Combines (corn, i.e., maize)	6,000	200

new equipment plummeted and the percentage of worn-out equipment increased. Thus in 1958–61 the total volume of agricultural machinery decreased for the first time in peacetime Soviet history. In the Russian SSR alone, there was a *deficit* of 420,000 tractors, 76,000 trucks, and 136,000 combines—all essential for optimal agricultural production. The kolkhozes had machinery for only 26 to 48 percent of the work power they needed.* Because of the shortage of mechanical aids, it took much longer to do most chores. There was a chronic lack of money to buy machinery, so the kolkhozes turned to the State Bank for loans, but could not repay them on time. Their debts to the bank grew steadily, reaching more than 2 billion rubles in 1961—more than the amount that Khrushchev had set in 1957 as the total value of all MTS equipment. Thus not only agriculture but also the entire agricultural equipment industry was now on the edge of ruin.

5. No adequate provision had been made for repair stations. When the machine-tractor stations were abolished by law, it had been envisioned ("envisioned" is the only word) that since there had been 8,000 such stations, somehow 4,000 state-owned MTS repair stations would be established. These repair stations were never established with any success and so, in 1961, it was decided to have repairs carried out directly on the kolkhoz. Only large kolkhozes—10,000 of them—could afford to

* *Razvitie sel'skogo khoziaistva v poslevoennye gody* (Agricultural Development in the PostWar Years) (Moscow, 1972), p. 339.

set up their own repair shops, but 34,000 had none and repairs were made in a haphazard fashion.* To prevent the abuse of agricultural equipment by amateur mechanics the government established technical service stations in selected farm areas. Many mechanics who had left the machine-tractor stations to work in the city returned to work in these centers—which was a positive development. But, in 1964, they were able to meet only half of the demands for necessary repairs.† And even in 1965, the total number of skilled mechanics on kolkhozes and the new repair stations was lower than the number employed by kolkhozes and machine-tractor stations in 1957.‡

These negative consequences of a "reform" that was so poorly planned and irresponsibly executed were acknowledged only later when there was some gesture toward lowering the prices of agricultural equipment, gasoline, spare parts, and trucks, but the discount was too insignificant to have much effect. Prices were still too high in 1964 after the second discount. In order to buy four tires for a small Belarus model tractor a farmer had to sell thirteen tons of wheat!

Thus Khrushchev's basic reform in agriculture was a failure that seriously reduced rather than increased agricultural productivity.

* *Ekonomicheskaia Gazeta* (Economic Gazette), April 6, 1973.

† *Ekonomika sel'skogo khoziaistva* (Agricultural Economics), 1965, no. 5, p. 30.

‡ Cf. *Narodnoe khoziaistvo SSSR* (The National Economy of the Soviet Union) for 1958 and 1965.

chapter nine

FIASCO
IN RIAZAN OBLAST

✡

PERHAPS the least known, but certainly the most tragic episode in the record of Khrushchev's agricultural and economic policies was the incredible "Riazan fiasco." Riazan is an agricultural oblast (area: approximately 18,000 square miles) whose capital city is about 115 miles southeast of Moscow. This hapless oblast was dragged into virtual bankruptcy through the political aspirations of its chief boss, as we shall see.

Khrushchev-watchers within the Party and state apparat knew that besides appointing to high office personal acquaintances and former associates whose loyalty he trusted, he also rapidly advanced those who had achieved notable success in agriculture or industry—innovators who at the same time followed Khrushchev's own line of thought. For example, G. I. Voronov, secretary of the Orenburg oblast committee, was named a candidate member of the Central Committee Presidium after Orenburg overfulfilled its grain quota. Voronov attributed this achievement to a "new agricultural technique" (no more cultivation after autumn plowing). This "new technique" proved ineffective in subsequent years—Orenburg's "success" lasted only one season—but by then Voronov was well on his way to the top and had been made agricultural inspector of the entire Russian SSR.

We have seen how Khrushchev's May 1957 speech goading the nation to overtake the United States in the production of meat, milk, and butter within three to four years had nearly cost him his job at the June Plenum in 1957, but the political conflict at the time overshadowed the problems of animal husbandry. Now Khrushchev wanted to deal with the charges of "irresponsibility" and "adventurism" and make his critics eat their words. He had to vindicate himself by proving that his goals were realistic and attainable. Thus it was obvious that any aspiring Party official seeking promotion could attract Khrushchev's favorable attention by outstanding achievement in the production of meat.

The modest rise in livestock output in 1957 and 1958 only made Khrushchev angry, for it seemed to provide his critics with evidence supporting their skepticism.

Apparently overlooked was the fact that, in 1957, the Soviet Union still lacked proper resources for any rapid development of animal husbandry. Although after 1953 the government substantially raised prices for livestock products, production costs in all agricultural regions had risen even higher. There were many reasons for the high cost of production—above all it was due to limited mechanization, the absence of large modern livestock facilities, and shortages of fodder. The government-set prices for meat to be sold at retail were low and, for political reasons, Khrushchev decided not to raise them. Thus, although in 1957 kolkhozes and sovkhozes were receiving more money for the sale of their meat to the government than they had in 1950–53, this higher income still did not bring in a real profit, without which there could be no increase in number of cattle bred. Under the circumstances additional livestock could only augment the financial losses incurred by the farms, and the majority, when assigned higher quotas for meat production, demanded subsidies from the government to achieve these targets.

In 1957 manual labor still predominated in the livestock industry. Only 5 percent of all the labor involved made use of machinery.* Thus it was unreasonable to expect a rapid growth of livestock products. In 1958, meat production had increased by a meager 5 percent,† whereas Khrushchev had demanded a rise of 60 to 70 percent!

This inauspicious beginning was unacceptable to the Kremlin leaders. All oblast committees were ordered to take decisive measures to show a substantial improvement in 1959. At this juncture, fired by ambition, A. N. Larionov, First Secretary of the Riazan oblast committee, made a very radical and bold offer. He firmly committed himself to more than double meat production in his region in 1959.

Such a promise was spectacular and for this very reason it attracted Khrushchev's attention and he guaranteed his personal assistance to help Riazan not only to attain its goal but even to surpass it. He made certain personal commitments to Larionov as well. (According to rumor, Khrushchev promised him the chairmanship of the Council of Ministers of the Russian SSR.) To this end, Larionov called a conference of regional activists in agriculture. In a state of euphoria, they made even higher pledges—the Riazan oblast would increase meat production five times on the kolkhozes, almost four times on the sovkhozes, and triple its quota for delivery and sale to the government. In 1958 the region had sold 48,000 tons of meat to the state, and now promised to have 150,000 tons to sell in 1959.

* *Voprosy ekonomiki* (Problems of Economics), 1963, no. 9, p. 97.

† *Narodnoe khoziaistvo SSSR v 1958g* (The National Economy of the Soviet Union in 1958) (Moscow: Central Statistical Administration [TsSU], 1959), p. 469.

The editors of *Pravda* did not want to report on these new Riazan goals and those on the Central Committee concerned with agriculture also opposed their publication, considering them to be grandiose and unattainable. However, on Khrushchev's direct orders, the pledges were printed in *Pravda* on January 7, 1959. Backed by such high promises from Riazan, Khrushchev now demanded that other oblasts follow suit and increase their fairly modest pledges. The Twenty-First Party Congress was scheduled for January 1959, at which the "Seven-Year Plan for Development of the Soviet Union" was to be presented, with a dramatically ambitious section on agriculture. Khrushchev wanted to ensure a spectacular success for the plan's first year. Under pressure from him, many oblasts began revising their figures. The Stavropol region undertook to increase its meat output by 150 percent in 1959, and the Krasnodar region pledged the same. The Moscow oblast and the Belorussian SSR promised to double production.

Khrushchev kept his word about giving particular attention to the Riazan oblast—he was full of praise at the Party Congress for the "wonderful start" made by the people of Riazan region. The oblast had barely began to try to fulfill its pledge when it was showered with awards and incentives. In February 1959, the oblast was awarded the Order of Lenin, and Khrushchev himself went to Riazan to confer it.

However, it was clear to even a casual observer that to increase the output of meat and dairy products or even the number of head of livestock so enormously in one year was simply out of the question. Nor was it possible to fatten animals enough and thus increase their total weight in so short a time. Since meat purchasing by the state usually began in the fall it was quite obvious that January was too late a time to start the whole campaign. But excessive publicity and Khrushchev's personal involvement made retreat impossible.

To increase Riazan's meat output by a factor of four or five at the packing plants, it would be necessary to decimate the herds and appropriate almost all the kolkhoz and sovkhoz cows and pigs, a criminal act in the eyes of Soviet law. Nevertheless, the Riazan oblast committee ordered that not only animals ear-marked for meat, but also milk cows and breeding stock were to be slaughtered. Thousands of cows and pigs were "purchased" by coercion from stock on the household plots of farm workers and then added to the oblast's herds. The oblast organizations often did not even pay the kolkhozniks cash, but instead issued receipts promising reimbursement in the future (and not at market prices either).

Even these measures did not suffice. Riazan farm managers had to buy cattle from neighboring oblasts, often traveling as far as the Urals. At markets and on farms in these other oblasts, Riazan representatives would purchase cattle for cash, and then in Riazan they would resell the cattle to the government at only one-third to one-fourth of cost. Funds intended for machinery, credit, and other purposes were illegally diverted to these pur-chases. And still the fivefold increase was not achieved. Officials in neighboring oblasts, also under pressure because of their own increased quotas, discovered the Riazan purchasing "raids" that were going on and ordered police roadblocks to seize the illegally purchased cattle from the Riazan "procurement agents," who then had to resort to smuggling their purchased cattle through at night, avoiding the main roads.

Next the indomitable Riazan oblast Party committee levied taxes payable only in meat. These taxes were imposed not only on farms or farmers but were set for all institutions, schools, and even police departments. Some people started raising rab-bits. At factories and offices, money would be collected, desig-nated workers would go to a store and buy the required amount of meat (at 1.5 to 2 rubles a kilo), and then the meat would be brought to a government collection station, where it was "sold" to the state (at 25 to 30 kopecks a kilo). Butter was treated in much the same way, sometimes circulating between shops and purchasers several times (because butter sold to the state could be delivered to the shops again after registration by procuring agents). As a result, meat, milk, and butter quickly disappeared from stores throughout the oblast, and the number of cattle dropped sharply by the end of 1959.

Riazan leaders, however, rushed to celebrate their "victory." On December 16, 1959, a few days before the regular Plenum of the Central Committee, a letter, addressed to Khrushchev, appeared in all major newspapers. The letter, signed by members of the Riazan oblast Party committee, the Riazan oblast Executive committee, and the Riazan oblast Komsomol committee, boasted that the oblast had completely fulfilled its pledges, had quadrupled meat production, and had sold the government 150,000 tons of meat, three times more than in 1958. Thoroughly carried away by their own charlatanism, they promised that the oblast would have even more meat to sell the state in 1960—180,000 to 200,000 tons.

In recognition of his overwhelming achievements, Larionov was made a Hero of Socialist Labor and presented with the Order of Lenin. The entire Plenum unstintingly praised Larionov, no one more so than Khrushchev. New paragraphs were inserted in reprintings of school textbooks describing the "glorious feat" of the Riazan oblast.

Accolades for Riazan and its leaders continued in 1960, but its agriculture was at the point of collapse. Herds of cattle, cruelly reduced by the demands of 1959, continued to shrink. Farmers, whose cows and pigs had been "temporarily borrowed" in exchange for a receipt, refused to work until they got either a cow back or monetary compensation at 1960 market prices (which had doubled or tripled since 1959). It was cheaper to give back the cows, so this time a cow went from kolkhoz herd to household plot. The kolkhozes' financial resources were exhausted and there was no money to cover bank

loans. Even work in the fields slowed down and a very poor harvest was predicted. Having the promised 180,000 tons to sell
the state was beyond discussion—the wretched oblast was in no
condition to sell the government even half its usual annual commitment—it could deliver no more than 30,000 tons of meat,
one-sixth of the promised 180,000. In addition, only 50 percent
of Riazan's grain quota could be fulfilled. In plain language,
many kolkhozes had been ruined.

It was no longer possible to cover up the debacle and at the
end of 1960 a special delegation from the Central Committee arrived to investigate matters. The delegation confirmed the
worst—Riazan agriculture was in a state of devastation. The day
before a scheduled plenum of the Riazan oblast Party committee, Larionov, Hero of Socialist Labor, shot himself at his office
in committee headquarters.

The imitation of "Riazan methods" inflicted heavy losses in
many other oblasts of the Soviet Union. The nationwide production of meat decreased by 200,000 tons in 1960 and only in
1962 did a tiny increase begin.*

The Riazan fiasco and its consequences dealt a damaging
blow to Khrushchev's prestige. The unfortunate slogan "to
surpass America in meat production in three or four years" was
scratched from Party handbooks and now served only as a topic
for jokes. In new editions of Khrushchev's speeches, the Leningrad oration of 1957 was either not included or his comments
about overtaking the United States were deleted. As-yet-unmet
production figures cited in other speeches were also omitted or
replaced by more realistic figures or simple calls for increased
production. This falsification did not pass unnoticed, although it
did pass without comment.

The "Riazan experiment," which spread nationwide in

---

* *Narodnoe khoziaistvo SSSR v 1962g* (The National Economy of the Soviet
Union in 1962) (Moscow: Central Statistical Administration [TsSU], 1963),
p. 309.

1959–60, had prolonged aftereffects. Even in 1964, Khrushchev's last year in power, meat production was lower than in 1959. The production of eggs and wool was also lower than in 1959.*

Per capita meat production, from 1957 to 1964, increased only from thirty-seven kilos per year to forty kilos. In the United States, in 1961, about one hundred kilos per person were produced. The gap between the two countries in poultry production was even greater. As an indication of how unrealistic Khrushchev's "three or four years" was in 1957, it may be pointed out that in 1972–74, Soviet meat production per person was still less than half that of the United States.

* *Ibid. 1964* (pub. 1965), p. 361.

chapter ten

THE SOVIET–AMERICAN HYBRID

AMERICAN industry and agriculture had always intrigued Khrushchev—and aroused a certain envy as well. In one form or another he attempted to apply to the Soviet Union much of what he found in the United States. It was indeed his admiration for U.S. industrial and agricultural achievements that to a significant degree determined his desire to improve relations between the two countries and to put an end to the cold war. The policy of "peaceful competition" was his major achievement in foreign policy, and the democratic transformations he wrought within the Soviet Union—above all the rehabilitation of the victims of Stalin's rule-by-terror—gave the United States and other countries confidence in the sincerity of his attempts to improve relations with the West. Despite periodic disagreements and tensions the shift he brought about in this direction remains his major contribution to human welfare, a contribution which outweighs his many shortcomings and miscalculations.

The comparatively minor and isolated instances of "Americanization" or "Europeanization" in everyday life, industry, and agriculture (described in chapter 4) were almost all successful and still prevail, but several major basic reforms, by which Khrushchev tried to adapt American/European principles of "free competition" and "self-reliance" to the centralized Soviet economy without altering the government monopoly or Party dictatorship, had adverse effects on a nationwide scale and brought the country virtually to a standstill. He did not succeed in making the Soviet variety of socialism "free" in the sense of permitting the development of free economic initiative, and his incessant feverish reorganization of persons, places, and things acted as a brake on national economic development rather than as a stimulant. Several of Khrushchev's attempts at establishing a Soviet-American hybrid merit discussion here.

INDUSTRIAL SHOCKS

Manufacturing consumer goods on a mass scale and filling the stores with hundreds of new products or models commonplace in other countries but not even produced in the Soviet Union was a challenging economic problem. The Soviet Union's centralized economic system, in which the production of any type of item—from safety pins to steam rollers—is controlled by the State Planning Commission (Gosplan) and is directed by the appropriate ministry or government bureau, worked successfully where major industry was concerned: the building of powerful turbines, military and civilian aircraft, ships, armaments, atomic and hydrogen bombs, reactors; or the production of iron ore, steel, coal, oil, wood, and other raw materials. But it was a different matter when it came to mass-producing hundreds of different types of consumer goods, ranging from apparel and stationery supplies to home furnishing and appliances —innumerable items—each required only on a relatively small scale. Here centralized management through Gosplan was excessively cumbersome.

In capitalist countries the government does not directly structure the nation's industry to the same degree and the economy is decentralized and self-regulating. Although the advantages of a socialist system were demonstrated by the Soviet Union when it rapidly transformed itself into an industrial super-state with a powerful heavy industry, it was not able to compete with capitalist economies in the production of consumer goods and services essential for a high standard of living. Attempts to solve the problem through the "classic" Soviet method of centralized management led to a proliferation of Moscow-based ministries and to the fragmentation of already existing ones. The central bureaucratic apparatus expanded, but there were no real economic benefits as a result.

The question was whether there should be a second New Economic Policy, whether small local industry should be expanded or even private industry allowed to arise if only to meet the demand for simple goods which had been overlooked by Gosplan but which were necessities in peasant households, for example, wagons, carts, wheels, sleighs, wagon shafts, horseshoes, pitchforks, oven tongs, yokes, charcoal, etc. But the thought of private industry could not be tolerated in 1956—it would have been too radical an economic reform, one that bordered on "anti-socialism."

Councils of the National Economy

To avoid a total upset of the established principle of state ownership of the means of production, Khrushchev proposed retaining centralized control over defense industries and other vital sectors of heavy industry but, in all other areas of production, especially of consumer goods, control by Moscow-based ministries would be eliminated; management would be delegated to the oblast level with special regional economic councils (*sovnarkhozy*) established in the oblasts. The work of these economic councils would be supervised by higher bodies similar to those set up for the major industrial areas of the country and, finally, by a supreme economic council. Such councils had existed in the 1920s, primarily for the development of local resources. It was expected that this system would bring management closer to production, decrease bureaucracy, and foster local initiative and competition.

Oblast Party committees welcomed the proposed reorganization as an enhancement of their powers. Previously they had been responsible primarily for agriculture, small local industry, and services. Now an oblast committee would control both the local economic council and all industry within the oblast's boundaries. However, the secretary of an oblast committee was not given authority over any giant state military or industrial complex if such be located in his oblast—their chiefs or directors were appointed in Moscow.

The new reform was assured enthusiastic support at the Plenum of the Central Committee, where oblast committee secretaries comprised a majority. The Moscow bureaucratic elite was against it, all the more so because thousands of ministry personnel would lose their jobs in the capital and would have to move out to the oblasts to organize the new economic councils, but in May 1957, after a month of nationwide debate, the new reform was passed by the Supreme Soviet and became law.

The Outcome

The complete reorganization of industry is, of course, a highly involved undertaking and should be put into operation on a nationwide scale only after several years of experimentation in a few oblasts at most. Analysis of the plan by the press was no substitute for an actual test. It was most unlikely that consumer goods production would swiftly expand as the result of such reorganization. In an industrial country like the United States, decentralization means independence from Washington, but it certainly does not involve state-by-state fragmentation or the subordination of industrial management to the bureaucracies of the separate states.

Among the small oblast councils there arose not so much competition among themselves as an exceedingly intricate network of bureaucratic relationships, for the sub-units of large industrial complexes were scattered over different oblasts and raions and were subordinated to various different departments. Thus, a tractor factory located within the jurisdiction of the Volgograd economic council became dependent in structuring its production on plants (formerly subordinate to the now defunct Ministry of Tractor Manufacturing) scattered throughout dozens of oblasts. Previously the director of a factory could coordinate his operations through the proper ministry, but now he had to deal with enterprises subordinate to dozens of different economic councils and an individual council would sometimes meddle in a factory's production plans and thus disrupt production of components needed by, say, the Volgograd tractor factory while ensuring supplies required by its own local factory. Anarchy was gradually taking over in production, hindering attempts at specialization. Many factories started to produce their own components, which previously could have been easily (and more cheaply) obtained from plants in other oblasts.

The system of regional economic councils improved operations slightly in small local plants and factories, but acted as a brake on the development of large and specialized industries. This became apparent in 1958, one year after the reform. In 1959 it was decided to "consolidate" the councils, that is, to establish one large inter-oblast council in place of several small oblast councils. For example, the Moscow Council assimilated the smaller ones of neighboring Kaluga, Tula, and Kalinin oblasts; the Novosibirsk Council absorbed the councils of all western Siberia, Omsk, Tomsk, Kemerovo, and other nearby oblasts. Above these combined councils, central councils were set up, for example, there was the Economic Council of the Ukraine or of the Russian SSR. Finally a Supreme Economic Council was established, but the problem remained unsolved. It was necessary to restore nationwide regulation of various branches of industry. State committees sprang up in Moscow for individual branches of industry and these committees in effect assumed many of the functions of the former ministries. Chairmen of committees were admitted to the Council of Ministers of the Soviet Union with ministerial rank. As a result, by 1963 the bureaucratic apparatus for "managing" industry not only had not been reduced, as had been intended by the concept of "decentralization," but had almost tripled. Instead of American-style competition, the evils of duplication, parallelism, and dissipation of responsibility were the result. The rate of modernization declined, the list of shortages grew longer, while warehouses were bulging with unsold, outmoded goods scorned by the consumer. Industrial management had been transformed into a labyrinth of interrelationships with multiple administrations and departments. One often had to wait months to get an answer to an urgent question about everyday procedure. Thus the "new system for managing industry" had brought the nation to an impasse, and there was no obvious way out.

THE REORGANIZATION OF SCIENCE

Somewhat more successful was the reorganization and "decentralization" of scientific institutes, begun on Khrushchev's initiative. Until 1953–54, almost all new institutes were established in the large cities, primarily Moscow, Leningrad, and

Kiev. Scientific bodies such as the mining, petroleum, fisheries, forestry, and oceanographic institutes were in Moscow, although clearly there could be only tenuous contact from Moscow with the specific branch of applied science. Khrushchev moved many of these institutes to areas where the relevant industries were concentrated. This undoubtedly was a forward step. The entire project was declared open for nationwide discussion in the Soviet press. This was a novel democratic gesture, but the press remained rather cautious in its examination of selected topics. During the Khrushchev era, small-sized towns specializing in science were developed near Moscow as well as in more distant regions—the best known are Akademgorodok ("Academtown") near Novosibirsk and Dubna in the Moscow oblast, but in fact about ten such towns sprang up—Pushchino, Obninsk, Chernogolovka, and others. This also was a response to the influence of the West, where small scientific and university cities (Cambridge, Oxford, Gif-sur-Yvette, Heidelberg, Berkeley, and many others) have, in some cases, existed for centuries.

Khrushchev somewhat simplistically assumed that scholars and scientists in the West work so successfully because they are peacefully isolated from the bustle and distractions of the big city, enjoy pleasant living conditions, and can concentrate all their attention on their scientific work. In the Soviet Union, the establishment of such scientific satellite towns 40 to 100 kilometers from large industrial centers was indeed a good idea, permitting an improvement in living and working conditions for younger scientists (older, established ones often did not want to leave Moscow or Leningrad).

Later these science-oriented towns attracted large numbers of the creative intelligentsia as well and became centers of dissent and independent political thought. During elections for the Supreme Soviet and republic or local soviets the percentage of negative votes in such towns became slightly higher than for the country as a whole.* Thus, beginning around 1968, the restrictions on the establishment of new scientific institutes in Moscow, Leningrad, and other large cities were relaxed. The quiet scientific centers were gradually transformed into sizable industrial towns with an admixture of the working class in their populations

AGRICULTURAL SHOCKS

On the basis of the extensive information he absorbed about American agriculture, the advice of his American farmer friends (the best-known was Roswell Garst, a farmer from Iowa, who often visited the Soviet Union), and his own observation of agriculture in America during his visit in the fall of 1959, Khrushchev came to believe that a farmer's independence in determining how his own farm was to be run was a major positive factor. He clearly realized that the U.S. Department of Agriculture did not have absolute control over the farmers but only influenced them indirectly by means of example, demonstration, recommendation, and advice. All final decisions were made by the farmer himself, the only person who could really know what was best suited for his farm. Thus inspired, Khrushchev undertook a complete revision of the process of agricultural planning.

Under Stalin, a kolkhoz or sovkhoz was assigned an exhaustive production plan which specified the cultivation of each indi-

---

* During such an election, voters have the choice of only one candidate for the vacancy. Although they cannot select the individual, they do have one option— to accept the candidate by dropping the ballot into the ballot box (it is not even necessary to write "yes" next to the name) or to reject the candidate, either by not voting at all or by crossing out the name before dropping the ballot into the ballot box. By this way voting, of course, is not "secret" at all, because to cross out a candidate's name, the voter must go to a special stall and perform the negative operation in the presence of the election committee before the ballot can be put in the box. Thus, as a rule, 99.8 percent of those voting vote in favor of the candidate, but in the science-oriented towns, about 1 percent will visit the special stall and cross out the name of the undesired candidate.

vidual crop, the size of deliveries expected by the state, the amount of payment-in-kind due to the machine-tractor stations, etc. This planning "from above" often took no account of local weather conditions or soil capability. But in a system where the kolkhoz was compelled to turn over its output to the state without payment and where the kolkhozniks earned virtually nothing for their labor, obligatory planning "from above" was the only possibility, since the interests of the farmers always lay in having a *minimal* production plan.

After the various reforms of 1953–54, which attempted to stimulate an interest in increased production, the Central Committee decreed that the state would retain its right to establish quotas for individual products, but the level of overall production, the amount of land under cultivation, the size of herds, and choice of farming methods could be decided by the kolkhoz itself. A kolkhoz thereby was given a definite "material incentive" to increase output because surpluses above deliveries required by the state could be sold at higher prices and the proceeds divided among the kolkhozniks in proportion to their contribution based on work-day units.

This new system incorporating a hint of "free enterprise" played a positive role in the agricultural successes of 1955–58. But from 1959 on, when the campaign was launched for the unrealistic Seven-Year Plan, the new planning system was abandoned and the farms were again burdened with detailed plans "from above" which specified the acreage to be sown, size of herds, choice of crop, and strains of plants and breeds of livestock to be used: schedules for planting and harvesting were imposed, the free sale of produce was banned, and directives were issued regulating the purchase of machinery and fertilizer.

Khrushchev tried to enforce a feverish rate of development by setting exacting production standards but, in actuality, this method yielded only negative results. For example, after the Riazan adventure, which also occurred on a smaller scale in other oblasts, kolkhozes were denied the option of determining which animals were ready for slaughter. They were forced to maintain in their dairy herds cows that gave no milk but still had to be fed—a kolkhoz chairman could be prosecuted for shipping unproductive cows to the meat-packing plant without official permission. Thus, within three or four years, 30 to 40 percent of the herds on some kolkhozes consisted of such non-productive or low-yield cows. On paper, the herds grew in size, but from the economic point of view, it was absurd to fulfill the plan in this manner.

The Fate of the Agricultural Ministries

Khrushchev wanted to do more than merely transplant the American system where the state had a mere advisory function. He therefore reorganized the entire governmental structure—including the agricultural ministries, the larger and middle-level agrarian institutes and colleges, and the experimental stations. Some elements of these reforms might have worked, but given Khrushchev's typical impetuosity the program as a whole could have led to disaster and, in fact did, to the extent that what was carried out contributed to agricultural failures in 1958–63.

Khrushchev decided, for example, that a ministry of agriculture should issue recommendations to kolkhozes only through experiment and example. Therefore it clearly had to have ready access to the land. So he ordered the Ministry of Agriculture of the Soviet Union to leave Moscow, move to a rural area, and set up a large model farm there, a kind of permanent agricultural exhibition of nationwide relevance. The Ministry thus lost its comfortable administrative offices in Moscow and had to transfer its entire personnel to the enormous Mikhailovskoe sovkhoz, 100 kilometers from the capital. In a parallel move, the Ministry of Agriculture of the Russian SSR was moved to the Iakhroma sovkhoz, 120 kilometers from Moscow. Agricultural ministries of other republics (the Ukraine, Georgia, Armenia, etc.) transferred to various farms in a similar way. All were under obligation not only to supervise agricultural production, but also to set up huge "model" farms where persons on official visits from farms in other parts of the country could observe all the latest agricultural techniques and then imitate them.

Shifting the ministries to the countryside took place almost overnight—no time was allowed to construct the necessary office buildings or housing. The offices of the USSR Ministry of Agriculture were located in the Mikhailovskoe sanatorium, and the Ministry's staff had to commute daily from Moscow in special buses over poor roads. Usually the trip took two to three hours each way. Visitors from other cities or delegates invited to various conferences also had to make the trip, staying at hotels in Moscow. In addition, all the staff members, from administrative heads down to cafeteria workers, had to devote some time to working in the fields, testing new types of equipment, and often performing the most basic chores, such as weeding, or digging potatoes. For the middle- and upper-level executive, this was quite an ordeal!

Within a year, more than 1,700 of the 2,200 staff members had given notice, and most senior positions were filled by new and underqualified personnel. The Ministry's contacts with other parts of the country sharply deteriorated—for several years it proved impossible to incorporate Ministry telephones into the central Moscow circuit. Therefore, to put through a call from the USSR Ministry of Agriculture on the Mikhailovskoe sovkhoz to the Ukrainian Ministry of Agriculture located on a sovkhoz near Kiev took several hours of negotiations through a number of different operators, and frequently nothing could be heard over the line when the connection was finally made. Annoyed by the failure of the ministries to transform sovkhozes into productive model farms (the Mikhailovskoe sovkhoz as well as other "ministerial" sovkhozes, like the Riazan oblast, had become a subject for jokes—the harvest from the "ministerial fields" was usually very poor and the cost of products raised by the labor of highly paid office personnel was too great), Khrushchev appointed I. Volovchenko, the director of a successful sovkhoz in Lipetsk oblast, as Minister of Agriculture of the Soviet Union, on the assumption that a director of a sovkhoz might be better at managing a ministry than a former minister was at managing a sovkhoz. For the same reason the ministers of agriculture of almost all the republics were replaced by directors of other outstanding sovkhozes. In Khrushchev's opinion, moving "practical men" into policy-making positions would improve the quality of agricultural management. Unfortunately this result did not follow. Managing a kolkhoz or sovkhoz involves rather different skills than directing an entire branch of production on a nationwide scale.

"From the Asphalt to the Land"

Khrushchev's relocation of agricultural institutes, colleges, and technical schools from the cities to sovkhozes or teaching farms in rural areas also was a failure. He had blamed the shortcomings of Soviet agricultural education on the fact that students were taught in the republic capitals and major cities and not in rural areas. He often alluded to the example of the United States and other countries.

Many of Khrushchev's criticisms of Soviet agricultural education were justified. Since the earliest days of Soviet power, higher and secondary agricultural education received heavy support from the government. From 1928 to 1940, the number of specialists graduating from institutions of secondary and higher agricultural education had increased from 11,000 to 40,000. After 1947, the number increased to 50,000 and reached 210,000 in 1959. Theoretically, in 1953, the number of Soviet citizens who were highly trained specialists in agriculture reached 1 million, yet only 96,000 were actually working on kolkhozes, sovkhozes, machine-tractor stations, and related enterprises.* After the early reforms improving life in the countryside, the situation changed and, by 1957, 280,000 specialists were working directly in agricultural production but, with the closing of machine-tractor stations, the figure again dropped.

The reluctance of many specialists to work "at the source," i.e., on the farms, was related to many factors—low pay (the salary of an agronomist on a kolkhoz, or that of a veterinarian, was seventy to eighty rubles a month, less than the wages of an unskilled urban worker), reluctance to become a member of, and hence tied to, a kolkhoz, the poor standard of living, etc. If an agricultural college or institute was located in a city it was easier for its graduates to avoid being assigned to work on a farm. (For girls, who comprised not less than 70 percent of the total number of students, the easiest way to avoid a rural assignment was to marry someone not a kolkhoznik.) †

Perhaps a long-term program of slow, gradual transfer of agricultural and technical schools from the cities to rural areas would have been feasible. There would have been time to erect modern buildings for classrooms and research, student dormitories and recreation centers, etc.—to plan for American-style campuses. But again Khrushchev could or would not wait or even consider the financial outlays involved. He insisted that all agricultural institutions be transferred to rural areas within two to three years. Neither the State Planning Committee nor the Finance Ministry could supply the funds needed for such an

---

* *Narodnoe khoziaistvo SSSR v 1958g* (The National Economy of the Soviet Union in 1958) (Moscow: Central Statistical Station [TsSU], 1959), p. 528.

† In the Soviet Union, a graduating student is given an obligatory three-year assignment by the state. The law does not permit him or her to resign or move on to a new position during this time. For a woman, marriage to an urban worker could be an acceptable reason for her to be allowed to stay in the city, but a man must go where he is sent.

exodus or the construction of necessary facilities—the buildings were not even at the planning stage.

But Khrushchev was convinced that problems would be minimal and, as in other instances, created examples to prove himself right. In the case of the Timiriazev Agricultural Academy in Moscow (which was the one nearest at hand), he simply forbade the admission of any new students as of 1961, thus reducing the numbers that would have to be moved when the academy was transferred to a sovkhoz in the Kursk oblast. (The Academy had about 7,000 students in 1961.) Plans for an agricultural college town 150 kilometers from Moscow and a marvelous design for a modern American-style "agricultural university" were worked out. The old quarters of the Timiriazev Academy, with its handsome buildings, laboratories, student dormitories, experimental fields, and a small forest, were designated to become the home of Lumumba University, newly established by Khrushchev for students from the developing countries of Asia, Africa, and Latin America.

However, neither Gosplan nor the Finance Ministry could underwrite the construction costs of the projected model college, estimated to be about 2 billion rubles. And the entire program of relocating agricultural educational institutions in the countryside would cost not less than 50 billion rubles—more than the government's entire expenditures for agricultural development over several years. Thus the program for shifting these institutions "from the asphalt to the land" remained a dream while those institutes, like Timiriazev Agricultural Academy, which had halted admissions since 1961, were dying a slow death. By 1963, the number of professors and instructors at the Academy equaled the number of students. With no new entering classes, and with a class graduating each year, by 1965 the entire Academy would have disappeared, had it not managed to outlive Khrushchev's reign. In October 1964, three days after

Khrushchev's ouster, admission of students to the Academy resumed.

A few agricultural technical schools, however, were successfully transferred to rural areas and when it was a question of constructing new technical schools or institutes, rural sites were automatically selected.

chapter eleven

THE AGRICULTURAL "MIRACLES" UNDER A CLOUD

IT was soon apparent that the abolition of the machine-tractor stations and the Riazan fiasco could not be viewed as glowing achievements that helped solve the problems of Soviet agriculture. There were two programs, however, that had been regarded as successful and were, perhaps, the cruelest disappointments that Khrushchev had to face when the true picture emerged.

TRIUMPH TURNS TO TROUBLE IN THE VIRGIN LANDS

The original triumph in the virgin lands was in fact rather different from Khrushchev's intention and desire. At the time when the campaign was launched, only a temporary use of these lands was envisaged. "Virgin land" is a relative concept: a newly plowed virgin layer of soil can be "virgin" only for four or five years, providing high yields as a result of nutritive substances already present in virgin soil. Under continuous single-crop cultivation, this accumulated supply is rapidly exhausted; thus, in the past, heavily plowed fields were periodically left "fallow" and not worked again for several years.

Khrushchev had assumed that grain from the virgin lands would wipe out the chronic food deficit in four or five years. By then there would have been time to improve agricultural conditions in the traditional crop-producing regions—chemical fertilizers, tractors, and other equipment would be abundant, and yields would skyrocket. As dependence on the virgin lands declined, it would be possible to shift from the exclusive cultivation of wheat to proper crop rotation. The overall program was that in time the usual kind of kolkhoz and sovkhoz would function in a normal way on smaller tracts of land, and there would be no need to rely on the annual mobilization of over a million additional workers—not only regular farm help but also students, office workers, truck and combine drivers (with their trucks and combines) from western kolkhozes and sovkhozes, and sometimes even army units as well—all of whom were sent thousands of miles from home to harvest the virgin lands.

In 1957, the gross yield of grain fell below the 1956 level by 25 million tons. * Kolkhozes and sovkhozes sustained heavy losses. This was particularly hard to accept after the spectacular crops of 1956. Throughout the Soviet Union all grain output declined in 1957. In 1958 the virgin lands produced a good yield and the total harvest of grain nationwide was 140 million tons—again setting a new record. Such fluctuations were natural since, according to long-range weather observations, climatic conditions in these eastern regions were suitable for wheat only two years out of five.

After 1959 it became apparent that the "virgin lands" would have to remain "virgin" and be exploited and relied upon to

---

* *Narodnoe khoziaistvo SSSR v 1958g* (The National Economy of the Soviet Union in 1958) (Moscow: Central Statistical Administration [TsSU], 1959), p. 436.

supply much of the nation's wheat for a long time to come. Plans to improve agriculture in the traditional regions did not materialize. With the early successes of the virgin lands harvests, Khrushchev had dismissed the idea of using the plan only as a temporary means of gaining time and instead cut down on financial and technical assistance to the usual crop-producing regions and even increased their financial burdens by forcing them to buy machine-tractor station equipment. Everything was poured into the virgin lands program but no parallel development whatever took place in the regular farming regions; their average annual grain harvest remained at the 1955 level and in some areas even decreased. As for the virgin lands, never again, despite an expansion in acreage, did they produce a harvest like that of 1956. Throughout the entire plan (1959–65) for national economic development, only in one year of the seven was the government's grain quota for the virgin lands met. The average yield of wheat per hectare for 1959–64 was lower than that for the previous five years (1954–58) which, of course, increased the unit cost of production. On the average, the cost of virgin land wheat was two to three times higher than that for wheat grown in the northern Caucasus, the Don region, or the Ukraine.

With more and more foodstuffs needed because of industrialization and the growth of the cities, to rely on the virgin lands for almost all the increase was quite risky—if only for the reason that weather conditions in the east were extremely unreliable. (This was to be proven heartbreakingly true in 1963, when there was a drought in the virgin lands, as will be shown in chapter 14.) If there had been large grain reserves this unreliability would not have been so serious, but there were no such reserves. In the European part of the Soviet Union annual grain production per capita in 1961–64 was lower than in 1913! The entire stock of grain produced in a given year was consumed that same year, leaving the government no surpluses with which to establish reserves. As a result, the country's economic situation was alarmingly vulnerable to unfavorable weather conditions.

The exploitation of the virgin lands, which had changed from a temporary measure into the permanent source of nearly half of the country's commodity grain, could also have been less risky if some attempt had been made to apply standard agricultural methods—a permanent work force and peasant population, proper crop rotation, animal husbandry, etc. But with periodic mobilizations of labor and equipment, recruited for a month or two during the harvest, this was impossible. The exclusive cultivation of wheat was carried on from year to year on more and more new land—42 million hectares at the beginning of the 1960s. This single-crop cultivation encouraged a heavy infestation of weeds, precluding any possibility of increasing yields or of applying fertilizers.

Another serious problem was soil erosion, which became an ecological disaster by the early 1960s. Earlier scientific research had already predicted this would happen and those in charge had been warned of the folly of plowing millions of hectares of open steppe lands unprotected by forest zones. But the drive to "open up the virgin lands" left no time to consider local soil conditions or topography, or to employ anti-erosion measures. Not only were fertile lands plowed, but also saline areas and large expanses of light sandy loams, which were soon blown away by the wind. No one had analyzed these soils before they were plowed, and agronomists were not consulted until 1965. The plowing technique used (with the top soil layer being turned over) was harmful for soils in these areas, particularly with single-crop cultivation, but other types of plows were as yet unavailable. It is not surprising that erosion, like the weeds, took over from the very first years of the campaign.

In 1955–60 several hundred thousand hectares had been

ruined by wind erosion, but since there were millions of hectares of virgin land, no one was alarmed. In the dry summer of 1962, however, wind erosion struck at several million hectares. In Pavlodar oblast alone, 1.5 million hectares were "blown away." * But this was only the beginning. In the spring of 1963 a substantial ecological disaster occurred. Severe wind storms (with winds raging up to 95 miles an hour) lifted millions of tons of fertile soil from the virgin regions and carried it miles to the foothills of the Sayan mountain range and to the base of other mountain chains. Dust clouds hid the sun for several days, irrigation canals were choked, and along some stands of trees drifts of soil more than two meters high were formed. Many towns and villages were covered with dirt, and from thousands of hectares the arable layer was so completely removed by the winds that the underlying bedrock was exposed. Precise data on the damaged areas were not published, but millions of hectares were involved.

In 1965, wind erosion again damaged thousands of hectares in northern Kazakhstan, in the Krasnoyarsk region, and in Tuva oblast. Only after these tragic natural disasters did the government seriously begin to concern itself with efficient soil management. It will take at least one to two centuries before the arable layer is restored to these areas.

Few people are aware that this forced development of the "virgin lands" based on the principle of extensive cultivation along with seasonal mobilization of hundreds of thousands of workers was directly responsible for delaying the resolution of a major long-standing problem—the rights of various Soviet nationalities.

During World War II, Stalin had illegally transported to the east (primarily to Kazakhstan, the Altai region, and northern

* *Ekonomika sovkhozov i kolkhozov tselinnykh raionov* (The Economics of Sovkhozes and Kolkhozes in the Virgin Lands Regions) (Moscow, 1964), p. 239.

Uzbekistan) several national minorities accused of collaboration (but not proven) with the invading Germans. The Kalmyks, Chechens, Kabardinians, Balkarians, Ingush, Volga Germans, and Crimean Tatars were banished from their homelands. After 1956 and the resolutions of the Twentieth Party Congress concerning Stalin, it was obvious that all these peoples had to be rehabilitated and allowed to return to their national territories. This was quickly done for the Kalmyks, Chechens, Kabardinians, Balkarians, and Ingush—who were sent back to their villages and settlements. But the rehabilitation of the Volga Germans and the Crimean Tatars dragged on until 1967 and they still are not permitted to return to their native regions. There is no legal basis for the inequitable treatment of these two nationalities—it is purely pragmatic expediency. The mountaineering Chechens, Ingush, and Kalmyks did not take to farming and were more trouble than they were worth to the local population; they continued to live their own half-wild way of life. Thus the local population was happy to see the return of these peoples to their native mountains and steppes.

But the Crimean Tatars and the Volga Germans were hardworking; even in exile they quickly built up fine agricultural settlements in the new regions, properly cultivated the soil, and did not bother their neighbors. With the beginning of the virgin lands campaign it was the Volga Germans (more than a million people) who comprised the basic *permanent* work force, especially as tractor drivers, mechanics, or in other jobs demanding technical skill. Without the Volga Germans, all the operations necessary in the annual agricultural work cycle simply could not have been carried out. For this reason it was declared "inexpedient" for the Crimean Tatars to return to the Crimea or for the Volga Germans to return to their small homeland—which had been purchased from Catherine the Great by their forefathers at a price higher than that paid to Russia by the far wealthier Americans for the whole of Alaska.

AFTERMATH OF THE CORN CAMPAIGN

Khrushchev's second agricultural "miracle," his corn campaign, was also doomed to failure. Because he saw what corn as a grain and silage crop had contributed to the development of animal husbandry in the United States, Khrushchev was following a good precedent when, in September 1953, he recommended increasing corn acreage in the Soviet Union. In 1954 the area under corn had increased to 4.3 million hectares and under more relentless pressure from Khrushchev, it increased to 18 million hectares in 1955. In subsequent years the acreage should have been held to this already excessively high figure and attention turned to methods of cultivating, fertilizing, and raising what was already planted of this alien crop, still a comparative novelty in many agricultural regions of the Soviet Union.

But Khrushchev, having put forward his program for tripling meat production, felt that only corn could guarantee the livestock herds he desired. Thus after 1957 he attempted, with redoubled energy, to establish corn as a common crop not only in the southern regions and central zone, where it sometimes gives satisfactory yields, but throughout the Soviet Union. He failed to consider that corn requires great inputs of labor, fertilizer (which was lacking), hot weather (found only in the Soviet south), and rich soil (not present either in Siberia or in Leningrad oblast). The necessary specific for corn cultivation—mechanical equipment—was not available nor was it in full production. Nevertheless, the area under corn grew steadily—whether the kolkhozes were in favor or not. By 1960 corn acreage had risen to 28 million hectares; in 1962 it reached 37 million.[*]

---

[*] *Narodnoe khoziaistvo SSSR v 1963g* (The National Economy of the Soviet Union) (Moscow: Central Statistical Administration Bureau [TsSU], 1964), p. 269.

Corn for Silage

These millions of new hectares planted in corn created major problems in those regions climatically unsuited for this crop (Belorussia, the Baltic republics, the central zone, the northwest oblasts, the Urals, Siberia, and the Far East). Here corn was, of course, not grown for grain, but for silage and by Khrushchev's estimates, should have yielded 300 to 400 centners of green vegetative mass for silage per hectare. But because of the lack of fertilizer, machinery, and manpower, such yields were rare exceptions. According to the Central Statistical Bureau, the average annual yield of green corn for silage was only 86 centners per hectare for 1954–58.* As for Belorussia, the central zone, and other northern and eastern oblasts, the yield of corn did not, on the average, exceed 50 centners per hectare. With such yields corn was totally uneconomical as a silage crop and distinctly less desirable than the traditional clover and other grasses, which do not require such great labor inputs.

In the years following, under heavy pressure from the Central Committee and local authorities, the methods used in raising corn improved, fertilizer became available, and some specialized equipment appeared (although inadequate). But corn yields for green fodder and silage remained too low in many oblasts to justify the labor input. In 1963 the nationwide average of corn for silage harvested was only 70 centners per hectare. In 1965, after Khrushchev's dismissal, average yields were still extremely low—a nationwide average of 98 centners per hectare. Economists had long since calculated that with silage yields of less than 100 centners per hectare, corn not only provides fewer "feed units" than other standard feed and forage crops but, if machinery is lacking, does not justify the extra labor necessary to raise it. And since in a situation of chronic labor shortages, it

* *Ibid. 1962* (pub. 1963), pp. 236–37.

was mostly factory and office workers from the cities who were sent "to grow the corn" (while retaining the pay-scale of their regular jobs), the unit cost of "green feed" from corn turned out to be especially high. It was calculated that in 1958–62 the growing and harvesting of 100 feed units of perennial grasses (clover, timothy, meadow grasses) cost one to three rubles, while the same 100 feed units from corn cost five to six rubles.*

But these calculations are beside the point—corn simply never was and still is not a reliable crop in those regions of the Soviet Union where it was then being introduced. Before 1962 one could validly argue that low yields were the fault of local authorities and kolkhozes who failed to provide the necessary labor, fertilizers, etc. But 1962 turned into a year of crisis—the spring and early summer were cool and rainy. For perennial grasses, now extensively supplanted by corn, it would have been an ideal summer. But corn, the hot weather crop, could not survive, and 70 to 80 percent of the acreage planted died.† In some oblasts a real "corn disaster" occurred; more corn had been planted than in other oblasts and almost all of it was killed. (In Vologda oblast, 58,000 hectares of corn were planted, but only 1,000 could be harvested.) The amount of corn silage procured for cattle varied greatly from oblast to oblast. In Lithuania, for example, in 1960, 6 tons of silage per cow had been stored, in 1961, 4.5, and in 1962, less than a ton. In Estonia, which had held out the longest against adopting corn, 1962 was very bad—only 300 kilos of corn silage per cow were procured, a tenth of the amount available in 1960.

Khrushchev's experiment of turning Siberia into a vast cornfield also ended in failure. Once in a while things went well, but frequently an entire fledgling crop was killed by late frosts in

* *Voprosy ekonomiki* (Problems of Economics), 1963, no. 2, p. 22.

† *Sel'skaia zhizn'* (Rural Life), newspaper, November 10 and 22, 1964.

early summer or maturing corn was struck down by early frosts at the end of August.

The infatuation with corn and the pouring of almost all manpower reserves into the cornfields inflicted indirect as well as direct injury. Lest the kolkhozniks turn back to their traditional haying fields, the government halted the manufacture of equipment for improving and maintaining natural meadows. Work on grass seed development also stopped. Brush and hummocks took over the hayfields and pastures, which then turned swampy. One-third of all meadowland was almost completely abandoned. From 1953 to 1965 in the Russian SSR alone some 6 million hectares of hayfield became overgrown and were no longer usable.* In other republics, where more than one-third of the hay was not mown for lack of equipment, it was necessary in the spring, when there was not enough fodder for the livestock, to "import" straw from the south.† The nationwide average annual production of hay dropped from 64 million tons in 1953 to 47 million tons in 1965.‡

Khrushchev had hoped that corn would solve the fodder problem in the central and eastern regions of the country, but after ten years of an uninterrupted campaign, the majority of kolkhozes and sovkhozes in these areas had not realized any profits, but rather had incurred increasing losses.

Corn as a Grain Crop

In southern regions of the country (the Kuban and the northern Caucasus, the Crimea, the south of the Ukraine) corn might have had a certain positive significance, especially if grown for grain. The grain corn harvest rose from 4 million tons

* Plenum of the Central Committee, March 24–26, 1965. Stenographic Record (Moscow, 1965), p. 48.

† *Pravda*, December 16, 1964.

‡ *Ekonomika sel'skogo khoziaistva* (Agricultural Economics), 1966, no. 3, p. 16.

in 1953 to 14 million in 1964. But this increase had been achieved only through extended acreage and not through high yields of corn per hectare, as was the case in the United States. After considerable effort, the average annual yield of grain corn was 14 centners per hectare, while winter wheat, with much less input of labor, had an average annual yield of 13 centners. In 1962, the wheat yield in the south was a bit higher than that of corn (16.8 centners per hectare vs. 16.6 centners per hectare, respectively).* By economists' calculations, a hectare of corn involved on the average a *loss* of twenty rubles; a hectare of wheat, a *profit* of twenty rubles. † Labor input per centner of corn was three times higher than the input per centner of wheat. Thus even in the south corn could not be considered an overwhelming success. In addition, the expansion of corn acreage meant that there was less acreage sown in winter wheat.

Khrushchev wanted to turn the northern Caucasus into a "corn state" and basically shift wheat growing to the eastern virgin land areas. He proposed the same idea for the southern Ukraine, the Don oblasts, and the lower Volga region. Perhaps if he had proceeded slowly, with the gradual introduction of corn, proper cultivation, mechanization of all operations, irrigation, and the use of inbred-line hybrids for seed and adequate amounts of fertilizer, a "corn belt" (like the one in the United States) might have been created in the Soviet Union. And there would have been corn yields of 50 to 70 centners of grain per hectare and 500 to 1,000 centners of green corn for silage. But in the absence of any cautious restraint, the "corn campaign" was basically a failure and only added to the nation's agricultural burdens.

Even before his enforced retirement, Khrushchev acknowl-

* *Narodnoe khoziaistvo SSSR v 1962*, pp. 269–70.

† *Planovoe khoziaistvo* (Planned Economy), 1964, no. 3, p. 53.

edged that he had made some errors in his "corn campaign." He was obliged to admit that corn was not always a profitable crop in all regions. When administrative pressure was somewhat lifted from the kolkhozes, corn planting dropped by 20 percent for silage and green fodder and 15 percent for grain. After Khrushchev left office, the country's "corn campaign" came to an end. The crop had become so unpopular during Khrushchev's time in office that in 1965 the amount planted fell below the 1940 level. Even those kolkhozes where it had been a success now refused to plant corn! Silage corn decreased at a double rate and the special corn store in Moscow had to be converted into an ordinary grocery.

chapter twelve

THE MEN
AROUND KHRUSHCHEV

DURING his years in power Khrushchev, like any other national leader, had many advisers who had no official role in Party or government. In many cases, he inclined to rely in great measure on the advice of these close aides rather than on the recommendations of members of the Central Committee Presidium or the ministers responsible for one or another sector of the economy. This by-passing of the Party/governmental hierarchy did not endear him to his colleagues and was to make him enemies.

In the early years of power, the creation of a comparatively unconnected group of personal aides helped Khrushchev map out certain programs or strategies, keeping them secret from Malenkov, Molotov, Kaganovich, and others he considered his adversaries. But after 1957 this modus operandi was no longer necessary and the constant shift of the controls of the policy-making machinery from the hands of the official Party and government apparat to those of an inner circle of advisers sowed the seeds of future trouble. Khrushchev traveled about a great deal, both within the Soviet Union and abroad, and often decisions were reached during these travels when only his own coterie was available for consultation. Thus it seems appropriate to consider here some of the men Khrushchev surrounded himself with. Because so much of his travels was concerned with agriculture, we will begin with one of the most controversial figures of Soviet science—T. D. Lysenko.

T. D. Lysenko

Sometime around 1956, Trofim D. Lysenko became one of Khrushchev's most trusted advisers on agriculture, in spite of some disagreements between the two during Stalin's lifetime. In the early postwar period, Khrushchev had had several confrontations with Lysenko, who was then President of the Lenin All-Union Academy of Agricultural Sciences as well as Stalin's chief agricultural adviser. Khrushchev had managed to get a number of Lysenko-sponsored schemes rescinded for the Ukraine. In 1947 he had emerged triumphant after a pitched battle with Lysenko and Kaganovich over the question of winter wheat vs. spring wheat in the Ukraine. In 1954 relations between the two became even more strained when Khrushchev discovered that V. S. Dmitriev, a one-time Malenkov Supporter in moves against Khrushchev in 1949–50 whom Khrushchev had fired from State Planning in 1953, had become Lysenko's closest aide.

Under Lysenko's direction, Dmitriev was engaged in pseudoscientific research on an attempt to transform one species into another (e.g., rye into wheat, etc.) by changing its environment. Mainly to discredit Dmitriev, Khrushchev scoffed at these notions as preposterous, but also took the opportunity to ridicule Lysenko as well. After the appearance of two articles in *Pravda* and *Kommunist,* making highly critical references to both Dmitriev and Lysenko,* the Ministry of Higher Education reversed

* *Pravda*, March 26, 1954 (article by Professor S. S. Stankov); "Nauka i zhizn' " (Science and Life), *Kommunist*, 1954, no. 5.

its earlier decision to award a doctoral degree in biological sciences to Dmitriev.

This decision fomented even harsher comments against Lysenko in the scientific press. He was openly accused not only of generating errors in theory but also of having sponsored many wrong and harmful recommendations concerning agriculture—of hampering research in corn hybridization, of unsuccessfully trying to grow winter wheat in Siberia, and a long list besides. The criticism was effective and Lysenko lost the presidency of the Academy of Agricultural Sciences. By 1956 his influence had dwindled rapidly.

However, he still had many backers in the Central Committee and in the Council of Ministers. In addition, two Khrushchev adherents and members of the Party Presidium coming to the fore, A. I. Kirichenko and N. V. Podgorny, were friends of Lysenko. (Podgorny was from the same village as Lysenko and was proud of this fact. Lysenko had been a famous scientist when Podgorny was still unknown.) Lysenko also managed to gain the favor of another of Khrushchev's trusted agricultural advisers, A. S. Shevchenko, by helping him become a member of the Academy of Agricultural Sciences. *

Exploiting these and other contacts, Lysenko worked assiduously to improve his relations with Khrushchev. Adroitly, he gave widespread publicity to everything Khrushchev proposed, describing his ideas with enthusiasm. Khrushchev, not surprisingly, was enormously pleased that Lysenko took it upon himself to press for fulfillment of Khrushchev's program for livestock development and that Lysenko had promised to increase the butterfat content of cow's milk throughout the Soviet Union in very short time. He also liked Lysenko's assertion that only small amounts of chemical fertilizers would be needed to

---

* Membership in a Soviet Academy means not only the honor and prestige inherent in the title, but also a substantial "academy salary" that can double the income of a scientist.

achieve high crop yields, providing these fertilizers were mixed with composted manure in a special way.

Thus, by 1957, Lysenko was restored to grace and managed to enter the select inner circle of the Khrushchev Set, accompanying him on many junkets around the Soviet Union. Without any education in agronomy and never having seriously examined Lysenko's bizarre theoretical ideas about heredity, Khrushchev quickly fell under Lysenko's persuasive influence and, in various addresses and reports, supported Lysenko in the latter's disputes with his scientific opponents. In 1961 Lysenko was reinstated as President of the Academy of Agricultural Sciences and M. A. Olshansky, his close friend and associate, became Minister of Agriculture of the Soviet Union (in ten years Khrushchev changed ministers of agriculture five times).

By this time, Lysenko's theories and programs had already been discredited in academic circles and agricultural institutions as well, and thus Khrushchev's intervention on debatable biological questions only reflected adversely on his own reputation. His agricultural advisers, in preparing his speeches, almost always inserted accolades for Lysenko and denunciations of those who opposed him. Often this criticism was rather blatant, but since many in the Central Committee, the Academy of Sciences, and the Ministry of Higher Education no longer believed in Lysenko's outmoded ideas, even Khrushchev's sharp attacks on an individual scientist did not lead to his dismissal. However, in 1959 Khrushchev—almost in a moment of pique—ordered the dismissal of N. P. Dubinin from the directorship of the Institute of Genetics in Siberia.

Dubinin was a long-standing critic of Lysenko. Despite Lysenko, he had managed to improve the quality of genetic research and established the Siberian Institute of Genetics at Novosibirsk. From its very beginnings this new institute had notable success in applying genetic methods to the selection of valuable strains—the development of triploid sugar beets with a higher sugar content, the use of radiation mutants, and other projects. Anxiously Lysenko tried in every possible way to discredit Dubinin and oust him from the directorship. But Dubinin lost his post through an unfortunate coincidence. Khrushchev was in the right place—at the wrong time.

In the autumn of 1959 Khrushchev had gone on an extended trip to the United States. Immediately after his return, he flew to China for the celebration of the tenth anniversary of the founding of the People's Republic of China. Mao Tse-tung had objected to Khrushchev's U.S. visit since at that time relations between the United States and China were extremely tense and the prolonged artillery duel between the Chinese People's Army and Chiang Kai-shek's army occupying the offshore islands was still going on.

The Chinese press completely ignored Khrushchev's American tour and a frigid reception awaited him in Peking. Traditionally, the leaders of Socialist and Communist Parties greet each other by embracing and kissing. But when Mao arrived at the airport to greet the Soviet delegation, he did not even extend his hand to Khrushchev. Discussions with the Chinese leaders were also strained and Khrushchev broke off his stay earlier than had been scheduled. He left Peking even before the conclusion of the anniversary celebrations (which admittedly did last for many days) and was in an extremely bad humor on his way home.

To cheer himself up, he decided to stop at Novosibirsk and visit its "academcity," then being constructed in accordance with his own ideas. However, upon hearing that Dubinin was the director of the prestigious Institute of Genetics and recalling that this same Dubinin was a "Morganist-Mendelist" and an opponent of Lysenko, Khrushchev vented his ill humor on Dubinin and ordered him to leave immediately.

Lysenko's pleasure at ridding himself of an enemy was short-lived. Within the same month, he lost an important ally, A. I.

Kirichenko, his No. 1 sponsor within the Presidium of the Central Committee. Kirichenko had been second-in-command during Khrushchev's trips abroad early in 1959 and had virtually run the government. That fateful year a good harvest was maturing in the virgin lands. When Khrushchev had left for the United States in the fall, he was fully confident that there would be a record grain harvest. But the beginning of autumn was very rainy, frost came early, and harvesting was extremely difficult—there were not enough grain dryers, there were not enough covered storage areas, there were not enough grain elevators. Not only was it extraordinarily difficult to reap the damp wheat, but the grain, with its high moisture content, began to germinate and heat up in the uncovered storage areas. The harvest was ruined. This disaster awaited Khrushchev upon his return from China. On Kirichenko fell the blame for the lack of preparedness. He was immediately dropped from the Presidium and dispatched to the Rostov region where, after a short time in the regional office, he disappeared into the obscurity of the raion level of activity.

Lysenko survived this setback and soon regained his former influence. In April 1963 Khrushchev directly intervened in a decision of the Lenin Prize Committee and forced the Committee to rescind its rejection of the candidacies of two of Lysenko's followers whose names had been put forward for Lenin Prizes. As a result of this pressure, the Committee voted a second time and the two Lysenkoites were awarded prizes.

In June 1964, an enraged Khrushchev was almost ready to reorganize the entire Soviet Academy of Sciences, when one of Lysenko's very close associates failed to win election to the Academy after speeches against his candidacy had been delivered by Academicians Sakharov (the future Nobel Laureate) and Engelhardt. It had been Khrushchev who had ordered that more vacancies in the Academy be created and reserved especially for scientists recommended by Lysenko.

At the end of summer 1964, a series of measures were under consideration in the planning boards of the Central Committee which would again have threatened the advancement of Soviet biology and genetics. Although the situation in agronomic science and biology was of course better than it had been in 1948, Lysenko's complete blocking of any up-to-date trends in the study of biology could be felt throughout the entire system of academic and research institutions. The teaching of genetics was not only confused but dated, and students at all levels, from secondary schools to universities, were still learning "Michurinist biology." Knowledge about ways to develop hybrids remained limited, and many techniques long employed abroad were not even known to Soviet specialists. Sophisticated statistical methods in evaluating the results of agronomic experiments had not been developed—which facilitated deception and the falsification of results by the unscrupulous. Even today it is difficult to imagine where these retrogressive trends in the development of biological and agricultural sciences might have ended, if there had not been a major upheaval in the nation's power structure in October of 1964.*

M. A. Olshansky

Lysenko's influence on Khrushchev was, as we have seen, so strong that Khrushchev began to rely more on Lysenko than on his own minister of agriculture. Subsequently, on Lysenko's advice, he named M. A. Olshansky, one of Lysenko's closest aides and disciples, as minister of agriculture. Olshansky's appoint-

---

* Lysenko, of course, was dismissed from all upper echelon policy-making positions after the fall of Khrushchev, but he remains scientific head of the Gorki-Lenin experimental station even today (1976). The station has several laboratories, 1,000 acres of land, and about 200 employees. At 78, Lysenko still enjoys yet another privilege granted to all Soviet academicians—no mandatory retirement age. (The record for longevity/administration was set by S. Scriabin, director of the Institute of Helminthology, who died in office (1972) at the age of 99.)

ment was accompanied by unprecedented publicity for such an event—along with the announcement a portrait of the new minister appeared on the front page of *Pravda* (usually ministerial appointments were reported in the back pages of newspapers in the "Chronicles" section). However, Olshansky did not last long in this post, as just at this time Khrushchev decided to move the ministry "from the asphalt to the soil" and the transfer of ministry personnel from Moscow to the Mikhailovskoe sovkhoz began. Olshansky was totally unprepared for supervising on a workaday level.

Khrushchev's tendency to rely on his own hand-picked aides extended to the areas of culture and international affairs as well. Three of his principal advisers, A. S. Shevchenko, V. S. Lebedev, and A. I. Adzhubei, enjoyed the greatest influence. Lebedev and Shevchenko were official aides of Khrushchev's, while Adzhubei was Khrushchev's son-in-law (the husband of his daughter Rada) and the editor of *Izvestia*. Adzhubei and Shevchenko accompanied Khrushchev on almost all of his trips abroad.

A. S. Shevchenko

Shevchenko was Khrushchev's closest aide on agricultural matters. He, in fact, wrote the greater part of Khrushchev's speeches on agriculture or prepared "impromptu" comments for Khrushchev to make at agricultural conferences. Newspapers received texts for publication only after Shevchenko had gone over them and thus the appearance in print of an address or "concluding statement" that had not already been tailored in advance would almost always be delayed five to seven days.

Shevchenko had begun to work with Khrushchev in the Ukraine just after the war and was his adviser for more than eighteen years. A scientist holding a candidate's degree in agricultural sciences and a specialist in the area of agricultural economics, Shevchenko was Khrushchev's indispensable companion in Moscow, on visits throughout the Soviet Union, and on all of his trips abroad, principally because of his phenomenal memory. He was always ready to provide Khrushchev with needed bits of economic information, to pinpoint persons and incidents that dotted their long-time association. If, for example, Khrushchev should somewhere come across a kolkhoz chairman or a raion secretary he might somehow have met before, he had only to ask Shevchenko ". . . perhaps I've seen this fellow before?" and Shevchenko would at once give a precise answer: "Yes, Nikita Sergeevich, on September 22, 1951, at a conference of outstanding agricultural workers in Smolensk oblast. You asked him about the local breeds of cattle." Thanks to his adviser's memory, Khrushchev often amazed people by addressing them by name and recalling past meetings.

Shevchenko was a driving force in the acceleration of Khrushchev's corn campaign. Shevchenko himself published a small book on corn and aggressively promoted this crop. In 1960–61 he attained such influence in the power structure that, if agriculture was involved, even a Presidium member was unable to get an appointment with Khrushchev without first clearing it with Shevchenko. This dependence on Shevchenko irritated both the ministers and the members of the Presidium of the Central Committee, who stood significantly higher in the Party or government hierarchy than Shevchenko.

When Khrushchev was deposed, Shevchenko was immediately dismissed from the staff of the Central Committee and subsequently was given a scientific post at an institute of agricultural economics.

V. S. *Lebedev*

V. S. Lebedev's contribution as an aide to Khrushchev had special significance because he was on the staff of the Council of Ministers, rather than on the staff of the Central Committee. Khrushchev consulted him in matters of the arts and literature. As a functionary of the Council of Ministers, he was technically independent of the extremely conservative Culture Section of the Party's Central Committee, although his office was located in the Central Committee building. Little is known about how Lebedev's association with Khrushchev began; it is even difficult to establish exactly when he gained influence over Khrushchev. For many, the extent of Lebedev's influence became apparent when he convinced Khrushchev of the necessity of publishing Aleksandr Solzhenitsyn's *One Day in the Life of Ivan Denisovich*. Lebedev was friendly with the poet Aleksandr Tvardovsky, the editor of *Novy Mir*, and it was through Lebedev that Tvardovsky succeeded in getting permission to publish the Solzhenitsyn novel as well as other extremely outspoken works.

Lebedev's association with Khrushchev grew out of Khrushchev's unusual habit of having literary works read aloud to him rather than reading them himself. The readings usually took place at his dacha near Moscow or during his vacations in the Crimea or on Pitsunda peninsula on the Black Sea coast. Lebedev was also a journalist/photographer and, along with a group of other journalists, would accompany Khrushchev on trips abroad. On his return he would fill Soviet magazines and newspapers with articles and photographs flattering to Khrushchev (sometimes these were published under a pseudonym).

In 1963, with the approval of Adzhubei, Lebedev invited Tvardovsky to Khrushchev's southern residence to read his satiric poem "Terkin in Paradise." Many writers from outside the Soviet Union were also invited to attend. "Terkin," a bitingly anti-Stalinist epic, also hit at many of the bureaucratic restrictions still in force in 1963. Khrushchev laughed with great glee during Tvardovsky's reading, obviously enjoying many lines in the poem which sharply lampooned various aspects of day-to-day life in the postwar period. The general sense of the poem was explained to those who did not understand Russian. Seeing Khrushchev's evident satisfaction, which they had anticipated, Lebedev, Tvardovsky, and Adzhubei asked Khrushchev in the course of ensuing conversation whether it was possible to publish the poem. In the presence of the non-Soviet writers, Khrushchev agreed unconditionally—"what possible objections can there be to satire—of course you can print it!" Adzhubei quickly began publication of the poem in *Izvestia*, without even sending it to the censor, a step that was mandatory for the publication of material of any sort.

In the same way, about a year before, during Khrushchev's vacation on the Black Sea, Lebedev had read aloud to him *One Day in the Life of Ivan Denisovich* in such a way that Khrushchev felt the impact of this very powerful work. After all, its subject was the nightmare of the Stalin camps, described by a former inmate—a nightmare that had been abolished by Khrushchev himself. If the Solzhenitsyn novel had been shown to Khrushchev earlier, in Moscow, just after Tvardovsky had submitted it for review by the Central Committee in the spring of 1962, Khrushchev could not have read it for lack of time, but would have had to rely on the opinion of the ultra conservative Central Committee ideologists responsible for literature. Lebedev, aware of this, waited almost six months for the *right* moment for the book to have the proper effect. On returning to Moscow, Khrushchev put the question of publishing it to a vote of the Presidium of the Central Committee and, after its members refused to resolve the issue, he scheduled a second session, at which he managed, after considerable pressure, to push through the necessary resolution.

Nevertheless, at the beginning of his years in power, Khrushchev himself had been extremely cautious and conservative where literature was concerned. This is reflected in his vitriolic attack on V. Dudintsev's *Not by Bread Alone*, by the press campaign waged in 1958 against Boris Pasternak, who was forced to decline the Nobel Prize in Literature under threat of expulsion from the Soviet Union. Khrushchev himself had even once condemned "Terkin in Paradise" at a 1954 Central Committee meeting when the activity of *Novy Mir*'s editors was under discussion. (The poem, written in late 1953, waited ten years for publication.) In 1961, Konstantin Paustovsky was harshly criticized in the Central Committee for the publication of *Pages from Tarusa,* a collection of relatively mild critical works. (Paustovsky was the editor of the collection.) *Tarusa* was not published in Moscow, but Paustovsky succeeded in getting it published in Kaluga. The second secretary of the Kaluga oblast Party committee, who had permitted publication, was dismissed.

Lebedev, thanks to his intimacy with Khrushchev, managed in many instances to support literary works, films, and theater productions which had not received the necessary stamp of approval from the literature, film, or culture subdivisions of the Central Committee. But even Lebedev could not completely isolate Khrushchev from conservative influence and thus Khrushchev's pronouncements frequently changed and were often contradictory.

A. Adzhubei

A. Adzhubei was a friend of Lebedev and like Lebedev worked for the liberalization of literature. Under the direction of Adzhubei and Lebedev and with their participation, an illustrated book was published after Khrushchev's trip to the United States in 1959, consisting of articles on Khrushchev and his trip. Khrushchev liked the book so much that he wanted to award it a Lenin Prize. However, the categories in which one could get a Lenin Prize did not include journalism, only literature, fine arts, and music. At Khrushchev's insistence the regulations of the Lenin Prizes were revised and a prize was established for "outstanding works of journalism." This prize was of course awarded to the group of journalists headed by Adzhubei who produced the book on Khrushchev's trip, *Face to Face with America,* and Adzhubei became a Lenin Prize laureate. In subsequent years no further Lenin Prizes in journalism were awarded.

Adzhubei accompanied Khrushchev on almost all trips abroad and gradually became his unofficial adviser on international relations. At the beginning of the 1960s and during the Cuban missile crisis, Adzhubei on several occasions acted as Khrushchev's personal emissary abroad, while neither Gromyko, the actual Foreign Minister, nor the Soviet ambassadors in the countries involved were informed of the details of these missions. Adzhubei was recognized by "those in the know" as Khrushchev's unofficial deputy for foreign affairs, and this could only provoke indignation and bitter resentment in the Ministry of Foreign Affairs, in the foreign division of the Central Committee, and in the Ministry of Foreign Trade. (Khrushchev disliked the Minister of Foreign Trade, N. S. Patolichev, because of his earlier association with Kaganovich in the Ukraine and bypassed him in all international negotiations, even those connected directly with trade.)

Gradually there formed around Khrushchev something like an "inner cabinet," a clique consisting of his closest advisers and associates, who operated quite independently of the Council of Ministers or the Presidium. P. A. Satiukov, editor-in-chief of *Pravda,* also became a member of this select group. Through *Pravda* and the principal picture magazines (which are subordinate to the editorial board of *Pravda*), Satiukov launched an intensive campaign to popularize Khrushchev as a "national leader"; the extent of these encomia soon exceeded what had been typical even for Stalin. Stalin had led a reclusive life, which gave little chance for the frequent publication of articles and photographs. But now photographs of Khrushchev engaged in various activities inundated the entire press, inevitably giving rise to talk of a "Khrushchev cult." As the "inner cabinet's" influence on important decisions and appointments was increasingly felt, Khrushchev's relations with members of the government and of the Central Committee of the Party steadily eroded.

chapter thirteen

"REFORMS" THAT STARTED A POLITICAL CRISIS

THE failures in industrial management and in agriculture were not the only ones to give rise to deep and widespread disappointment and doubts about Khrushchev's competence as a Party and government leader. The decline of confidence was strongly accelerated by other new programs, some of which were designed to change the Party structure and its role in Soviet society and others to reorganize the entire secondary school setup. All of these so-called reforms were rooted in good intentions—liberalizing the rigid Party apparat, or bridging the gap between educational ideals and economic necessity, but again the speed of transformation led to negative consequences.

Clearly the Soviet Union's general education system needed reform after Stalin's death and one change, made in 1954/55—the elimination of separate schools for boys and girls—met with success. However, this reprograming of the secondary school system, carried out on a nationwide scale, involved also a shift from the traditional ten-year program to an eleven-year "polytechnical" one that was hotly resented by both urban and rural residents. Under the new plan, boys and girls, beginning at fourteen or fifteen years of age, were required to learn some manual trade (e.g., that of lathe operator, metal worker, tractor driver, textile worker, etc.); schools were affiliated with the nearest factory, plant, repair shop, kolkhoz, or sovkhoz, whose workers were required to turn themselves into craftsmen-teachers. One full day a week (or twice a week for several hours), pupils did not report to school, but went to various departments of a factory or to a sovkhoz or kolkhoz to work, where they were instructed in some kind of vocational skill. All this necessitated sizable financial investment and created problems both for the industrial enterprises and for the schools.

Factory workers grumbled about having to spend time teaching schoolchildren various simple skills in addition to meeting their own production quotas, while students and parents were dissatisfied because they could not choose the trade to be learned—usually it was determined by the nature of the nearest suitable industrial enterprise. The majority of students felt that they would never actually use the skills they were being forced to acquire. Subsequent statistics showed that the students were right—95 percent did not make use of their required "professional" training after graduation, but rather tended to work in other jobs, or enroll in a technical school or a university. Still, despite objections, Khrushchev insisted on strict compliance with his educational "reform," which was approved by the Supreme Soviet and became an obligatory law.

A certain loosening of regulations imposed on the Soviet nationalities groups led to a growth in nationalism,* which

* Less than 50 percent of the population of the Soviet Union is ethnically "Russian." There are more than a hundred other national groups. The major ones have a restricted autonomy in the form of a National Soviet Republic (e.g., Estonia, the Ukraine, Georgia, etc.) in the geographic areas that have belonged to them for centuries. All of these individual nations were "inherited" from the old

frequently complicated centralized direction and sometimes was detrimental to progress in science and technology. For example, after the relaxation of the single language (Russian) requirement, many scientific journals throughout the Union Republics were published in the local language; mathematicians, chemists, and biologists described their experiments in Armenian, Georgian, Belorussian, Ukrainian, or other languages of the fourteen national republics. This meant a waste of scientific information—Russian scientists, for example, could not avail themselves of information described in a technical or scientific article written in Ukrainian, not to mention Georgian or Estonian. Nor could these minority language groups read each others' publications. This nationalist tendency ran counter to the process of international scientific integration, which has led to the worldwide use of major languages (English, German, French, or Russian) and to the voluntary abandonment of minor languages on the part of small countries (Swedish, Dutch, Hungarian, etc.) in specialized scientific and technical publications.

The need to curb government spending in one area to create funds for another forced Khrushchev to abolish the pay differentials paid to workers in Siberia, the north, and Far East, which not only caused dissatisfaction there but also led to a gradual population drift away from these economically important areas. A limited monetary reform carried out in 1961 was also unpopular (the purchasing power of the ruble was increased by a factor of ten and all wages and prices were simultaneously reduced by the same factor). Prices were sometimes then reestablished at a higher level. Disappointed with the slow growth in labor productivity, Khrushchev tried to get production

---

Russian empire, either joining or being conquered by Russia at different times during the fifteenth to twentieth centuries. Some nationalities, like the Uzbeks, Latvians, Armenians, and Georgians, possess cultures and languages older than the Russian one; many have different religious backgrounds—Moslem, Roman Catholic, etc.

norms and pay scales revised in many branches of industry, which caused serious worker discontent and much labor tension. The failure to increase meat production, compounded by the Riazan affair, reduced state meat resources and forced the government to raise the retail prices of meat, butter, milk, eggs, and other products as much as 50 percent. In some places these increases were not accepted meekly and there was open conflict between officials and angry consumers. As a result, Khrushchev's popularity in 1961–62, which had been based on his successes during 1953–58, plummeted as he and his aides were well aware. A general mood of dissatisfaction permeated the entire Party network.

Sensitive to the cold winds of changing public opinion, Khrushchev once again used the old ploy of denouncing Stalin. At the Twenty-Second Party Congress in 1961 he made public a number of shocking documents revealing crimes against humanity committed by Stalin and his partners—this time Molotov, Kaganovich, Malenkov, and Voroshilov were named, all of whom had been passed over by Khrushchev in his speech at the Twentieth Party Congress in 1956.

The main objective of the Twenty-Second Congress was the adoption of the new Party Program and the preliminary version of Khrushchev's speech that had been approved by the Party Presidium did not include any mention of these new and even more shocking disclosures of Stalin's crimes. The speech was to be delivered in the open, not behind closed doors like in 1956, and nobody expected any dramatic twists. The revelations about Stalin set forth in the 1961 speech were even more shattering and on a much wider scale. Khrushchev told not about thousands of victims as he had at the Twentieth Congress, but about millions, with stunning details about Stalin's personally signing hundreds of death warrant *lists*. After this speech and subsequent open discussions of Stalin's cruel abuses of power, it was no longer possible to clothe his name with any vestige of honor as had been done after the Twentieth Congress because of pressure from the Chinese Communists and as a concession to Party conservatives. Stalin's name and place in history were irreversibly compromised.

Stalin's embalmed body was removed from the Mausoleum on Red Square * and buried in a small cemetery near the Kremlin wall, while throughout the land all portraits of and monuments to the former leader were destroyed. Geographic locales, institutions, or organizations named after him were redesignated accordingly. Stalingrad, the famous city where the course of World War II turned against Germany, was renamed Volgograd.

These denunciations, in the opinion of some Western experts, were basically intended as an act of defiance against China's top leaders, who were constantly demanding that the Soviet Party restore Stalin's prestige and historical pedestal. Some senior Soviet officials believed that the denunciations of tyranny and the mode toward liberalization that followed them would weaken the position of the Chinese leadership in the international Communist movement. However, behind all these changes there also lay an attempt by Khrushchev to shore up his own reputation and popularity, and in political terms he did succeed.

For the Soviet intelligentsia, this liberal trend was seen in the permission to publish in November 1962 *One Day in the Life of Ivan Denisovich,* the novel by Aleksandr Solzhenitsyn about Stalin's labor camps, as well as some other works and memoirs by former prisoners. These appalling publications, distributed in millions of copies at the beginning of 1963, were widely hailed as the beginning of the freedom of the press.

But Khrushchev and his Presidium colleagues quickly realized that any wave of liberalism might be dangerous for themselves as well; it could threaten the monopolistic position of Party bureaucracy, and lead to other democratic innovations, perhaps even the modification or abolition of pre-publication

* Before the end of the Congress, on the night of 31 October 1961, near the Kremlin wall an excavator dug a deep pit, and Stalin's coffin was lowered into it. To prevent exhumation, the pit was filled with concrete, and a granite slab was placed on top. In Red Square the next day, the big gold plate with Lenin's and Stalin's names had been repainted and only Lenin's was left.

censorship for works of literature. In late 1962, while visiting a Moscow art exhibit Khrushchev vociferously condemned modern trends in art. When he, in typical peasant terms, likened the exhibition to "dog droppings" and demanded to know "who is responsible for this," renowned Soviet sculptor Ernst Neizvestny stood his ground and answered the Soviet leader firmly. He hotly defended modern art, telling Khrushchev that what he saw was far superior to what had been produced in Stalin's time. Khrushchev is supposed to have answered him, "You're the kind of man I like." Although a subsequent special "ideological" Plenary meeting of the Party Central Committee in June 1963 put a ban on liberal tendencies in art in favor of "socialist realism," Neizvestny was later commissioned by the Khrushchev family (at Khrushchev's earlier request) to create the abstract tombstone that marks Khrushchev's grave in Novodevichi cemetery (see chapter 15 and illustration). *

Already at a meeting with prominent artists, poets, and writers in March 1963, Khrushchev retreated from the anti-Stalin position proclaimed at the Twenty-Second Party Congress. Again he justified Stalin's actions up to 1934, saying that there must be due recognition for "Stalin's contributions to the Party and to the Communist movement. Even now we feel that Stalin was devoted to Communism, he was a Marxist, this cannot and should not be denied." In the same speech, Khrushchev accounted for much of Stalin's ruthlessness by saying that in the last years of his life Stalin was a sick man, suffering from chronic suspicion and a persecution mania. Aware of Stalin's pathological distrust and susceptibility to suggestion, the intelligence agencies of capitalist countries "fed him" documents and accounts that appeared to be authentic and he became convinced that "certain military experts within the country were

---

* Still persecuted for his art, Neizvestny applied for an exit visa and left the Soviet Union in March 1976. The Khrushchev family is storing such sculpture as he could not take with him.

operating against Soviet power and the Soviet state, and that plots were being hatched by various criminal factions." *

Following this semi-rehabilitation of Stalin, the censorship of literary works, far from relaxing, indeed became more stringent, and liberal members of the intelligentsia were increasingly harassed. Thus Soviet liberals grew disillusioned with Khrushchev since he obviously intended to revert to a tighter internal political course. "Ideological vigilance" and "the threat of imperialism" once again entered the everyday vocabulary of propaganda. In conjunction with the failures in agricultural production and increased burdens laid on peasants and workers, this new policy almost completely discredited Khrushchev within the Soviet Union.

Again there was an atmosphere of tension and a fear that the old ways of repression and terror could return. The authors of this book, at any rate, became apprehensive about their own fate; the manuscript exposing the crimes and charlatanism of Lysenko, which circulated widely among the intelligentsia under the title *Biological Science and the Cult of Personality* (Zhores Medvedev), had been severely criticized at the Ideological Plenum of the Central Committee in June and by *Pravda* in August 1963; while the initial, short version of the manuscript on Stalinism (Roy Medvedev), completed at the end of 1963, was already in *samizdat* circulation for comments and criticism.

Khrushchev also lost popularity with the military, largely as a result of his sudden unilateral action reducing the Soviet Army to 1.2 million men and cutting the military budget. It was not an ardent desire for peace that dictated this policy. Khrushchev needed that manpower and money to develop agriculture and industry. But in the opinion of the military, such a major unilateral reduction of Soviet armed forces inflicted severe damage to the nation's defense capability. The cuts also meant that thou-

* *Pravda*, March 10, 1963.

sands of career officers were prematurely retired on pensions and for reasons of economy, Khrushchev reduced the size of the pensions which, of course, infuriated those affected.*

Although aware that not only his own popularity but also the prestige of the Party was diminishing, Khrushchev incredibly stepped up antireligious propaganda. Churches were closed in many areas or, even worse, turned into garages in rural districts where there were not enough buildings suitable for storing agricultural equipment. Borovsk monastery, the third most ancient one in Russia and a famous architectural landmark which had been preserved as a museum, was transformed into a technical school for teaching the mechanization of agriculture; the rich murals in its chapels were obliterated with ordinary white paint.

Of the Soviet Union's total population, there were at least 50 to 60 million practicing Christians, primarily rural residents of the older generation. The closing, conversion, or destruction of their churches gave these people less reason for staying in their villages and added to the number of elderly people who left the kolkhozes (and on many kolkhozes people of retirement age formed a significant part of the labor force) to live with their children in the cities. The regulations preventing rural residents from moving to the city could not be applied to people of retirement age (fifty-five for women, sixty for men) who were joining grown children working in industrial or office jobs, because an old person in a rural area did not receive a state pension, and his or her social security had to be taken care of by the kolkhoz budget. As many kolkhozes were not able to pay a regular pension, they preferred to let old people go to their children.

Persecution of various religious sects and particularly active religious groups increased, especially after the enactment of the

* Khrushchev's decision to reduce the army and military budget also induced an open confrontation with the top military command. He soon received a memorandum from the marshals of all military forces, demanding that the army cuts be restored and warning of grave consequences for defense capabilities. The memorandum angered Khrushchev, but he finally retreated and halted the demobilization.

new Criminal Code of the Russian SSR in 1961, article 227 of which declared criminal any religious activity that might cause citizens "to reject socialist activity or the performance of their duties as citizens," as well as "the enticement of minors into a [religious] group." Thus, in addition to the separation of church and school—a measure enacted immediately after 1917—parents were now forbidden to give their children religious instruction at home, and charges could be brought against priests if young people under eighteen attended their services.

But it was not his economic and administrative blunders that created a gradually hardening determination on the part of Khrushchev's one-time adherents to switch their loyalties and attempt to replace him; much more important were two *intra-Party* structural changes. These were at first supported by the Central Committee, but later, in their practical application, turned out to be incompatible with the basic principles of a one-party system. These reforms caused the loss of majority support not only in the Presidium of the Central Committee, but in the general membership of its Plenum—particularly among the secretaries of the oblast committees, who represented a majority of the Central Committee Plenum.

The vivid portrayal of the cruel and arbitrary actions of the Party elite during the Stalin period, attributed (quite correctly) to the violation of democratic principles within the Party, enabled Khrushchev to modify Party rules, as well as to recast its program. Under the new rules, applicable to governing Party bodies (i.e., raion and oblast committees, and even the Central Committee itself), it became mandatory for *one-third* of the members of each committee to be replaced by new Party workers at the next election. * This theoretically applied to the Presidium of the Central Committee as well, although it did not extend to the First Secretary (Khrushchev), or to certain "experienced Party workers of special merit," who were also ex-

---

* Elections for Party oblast committees are held every two years; those for local committees are held every year.

empt. In a way this revision of Party rules introduced elements of democratization into the Party structure by depriving long-time office holders of what frequently had become life tenure and giving others a chance. The position of secretaries of oblast committees and secretaries of Union Republic Central Committees certainly was undermined, as the new rules meant a periodic evaluation of their performances in office, and gave them reason to fear replacement by younger blood. Any Party secretary, whether in charge of a republic, oblast, city, raion, or factory, wants to retain his position, unless of course it is a question of moving *up* the Party ladder.

Party posts, starting with those in organizations with over 500 employees, can be held by a full-time secretary or Party organizer, often selected from the ranks of employees, who receives a Party salary and soon can become a professional Party worker. Thus only the Party secretary in, for example, a small scientific institute, whose Party work is an added responsibility bringing no extra income while consuming considerable amounts of time, would be content to relinquish the post to someone else at the end of the term. But even the secretary of a raion committee is highly remunerated, and the prospect of being forced to give up the position after one or two terms in office could only be unpleasant. It was even more difficult to make the plan palatable for secretaries of oblast committees or for permanent members of the Central Committee.

The new rule deprived most members of the Central Committee of the sense of stability and security they so needed, while it enabled Khrushchev to shuffle Party personnel, remove those he disliked, and keep others completely docile and subordinate. Thus an undercurrent of tension arose between Khrushchev, who had in the past found the Central Committee Plenum as his chief support, and the secretaries of the oblast committees, who in large measure formed its membership. These frictions would have to be resolved before the next Party Congress, that is, by 1965, when the question of compulsory replacements of one-third of the membership of the Central Committee would have to be faced.

The second Party innovation, which perhaps provided the strongest incentive to those thinking about Khrushchev's ultimate removal, was the splitting of all oblast-level Party committees into industrial and agricultural sectors. This division was adopted at an expanded plenum in November 1962, although rightfully only a Party Congress had the power to enact such a radical reorganization of Party structure.

To a certain extent, Khrushchev was only attempting to extricate the nation from the impasse he himself had created by setting up the complex system of economic councils and by moving ministries of agriculture out to the countryside, which made them inefficient. The nationwide trend toward disorder, confusion, and lack of authority in both agricultural and industrial production, with an attendant decline in output, forced Khrushchev to seek a way out—not in cautious retreat to the more or less proven centralized method but by overhauling the entire Party system.

Under the existing set-up an oblast Party committee (together with the executive committee of the oblast soviet system) * was in complete control of the oblast, and the first secretary of the Party committee was the oblast's undisputed master. The second secretary was responsible for agriculture. But now, in the fall of 1962, every oblast party committee was split into an agricultural and industrial committee, each independent of the other. The oblast soviet executive committee was also corre-

* An oblast Party committee is a part of the All-Union Party network while an oblast executive committee is a part of the government network of soviets and in fact represents so-called "soviet power." However, the priority of power in an oblast as well as in the whole Soviet Union is in the Party system.

spondingly split in two. The principle of administration by territory had thus been replaced by administration by category of production.

It is difficult to say how industry was affected, but agriculture staggered under new burdens. The agricultural committees had few financial and organizational resources and the countryside's need for manpower from the cities intensified. The agricultural Party committees had no power to recruit urban factory or office workers for seasonal agricultural labor. The oblast industrial committees, now free of responsibility for agriculture, were no longer interested in lending thousands of blue- and white-collar workers to mow hay, bring in the harvest, or dig potatoes and gather other vegetables and, without this traditional assistance, agricultural tasks were endless. Many crops simply rotted in the fields.

Government-inspired articles began appearing in the newspapers preaching the need to increase kolkhoznik productivity and insisting that there *was* in fact a sufficient labor force in the countryside,* but these pieces had little effect. The contraction of labor supply from the city could not be compensated for by increasing kolkhoznik productivity. Pressure on the kolkhozniks was intensified and new bans and restrictions were imposed, especially on the use of household plots and personally owned livestock. But nothing helped.

There was also a division of functions in the central Party structure, both for the individual republics and for the Soviet Union as a whole. A Central Committee Bureau for Industry and a Central Committee Bureau for Agriculture were es-

---

* True—in the sense that compared to the United States and Western Europe, a much larger proportion of the Soviet Union's population *does* live in rural areas; but the majority of villagers are either war widows, old people, or those permanently incapacitated by the war. World War II left about 15 million widows and more than 20 million permanently incapacitated, mostly from the countryside. The majority of workers were immune from army service because industry was converted into military production.

tablished. Although at the top these "bureaus" were subordinate to one head—Khrushchev—virtually the entire Party structure was now divided into two independent constituents. Something remotely like a two-party system had emerged, still unified by a common ideology and platform, but with all the potential problems of such a system.

With the splitting of the oblast committees into agricultural and industrial sectors, the raion-level structure for directing agriculture, which had developed in the course of decades, completely altered. As geographical units of an oblast, raions were consolidated and existing raion Party and soviet committees were eliminated. Territorial kolkhoz/sovkhoz administrative units were established to direct production, the Party committees of which assumed the functions of the former Party committees of the rural raions. Raion soviets were also created in the consolidated districts, but the executive committees of these soviets had only limited functions and were not responsible for production.

The impact of this consolidation can be judged from the following figures. In the Russian SSR before the consolidation, an average raion had 37,000 inhabitants and twelve kolkhozes. After 1963 it had 68,000 inhabitants and twenty-four kolkhozes. In the Ukraine, an average new raion had 100,000 inhabitants, as compared to 49,000 in the old raion.* With the inadequate road network and poorly developed communications system, the sudden nationwide establishment of new raion centers, now often far away from their kolkhozes, caused a breakdown in communications. Often, merely traveling to the new center presented a tiresome obstacle both for the ordinary resident who might need some kind of permit and for the kolkhoz or sovkhoz administrators.

The first secretaries of the oblast committees, who had pre-

* *Kommunist*, 1965, no. 1, pp. 121–22.

viously exercised supreme power within their own regions, now lost this preeminence. In many cases, it was not clear just who was in charge of the oblast—the secretary for industry or the secretary for agriculture, for they functioned independently and were both *directly* accountable to the Central Committee, one to the Bureau for Industry, the other to the Bureau for Agriculture. The question became a very sore point. Someone after all still had to be in charge.

Under the old system, when a local Party official was elected to the Central Committee, it had always been the one and only "first" secretary. Now in some oblasts the industrial secretary had superior standing as former first secretary of the oblast, while in others it was the agricultural secretary, especially if he (or she) had had an agronomic education. An agricultural secretary who had been a member of the Central Committee Plenum might consider himself top person in the oblast, but the industrial counterpart might not acknowledge this claim. By tradition, the oblast committee secretary was also elected as representative to the Supreme Soviet of the USSR or at least of the Russian SSR. The chairman of the executive committee of the oblast soviet was also elected to the Supreme Soviet. This meant that now there were in all *four* possible contenders per oblast but, because of population ratios set by the Constitution (one representative per 300,000 people), not every oblast was entitled to have four representatives in the Supreme Soviet. To complicate matters further, there was a fifth person who also had a claim to be elected—the top-ranking worker or kolkhoznik in the oblast.

Naturally there was intense rivalry between the heads of oblast Party and soviet committees. This rivalry did not mean that democracy was in full bloom, with the people electing the "better" man, but it was democracy in embryo in the sense that a certain competition existed where previously there had been none. The oblast committee secretary ceased to be king in the region—he was only an industrial or an agricultural boss. Which secretary's opinion would carry weight with the public prosecutor or an oblast judge? Which would issue orders to the chief of police? Conduct the oblast's ideological conferences? Direct public health services? Education? Had not the Party of Workers and Peasants been divided into two parties—the Party of the Workers and the Party of the Peasants? Even the oblast newspapers would have to be separated into urban and rural ones.

Under the new system of management, neither industry nor agriculture flourished. Oblast committee secretaries, the backbone of the Central Committee, who had once enthusiastically supported Khrushchev because his early innovations had enhanced their status, had now come to bitterly oppose him. The existence of two Bureaus of the Central Committee—one for agriculture and one for industry—diluted the power of the Presidium and thus its members also turned against Khrushchev. Reversal of the entire reorganizational process could not be deferred until the next Party Congress, that is until 1965. Dissension within the Party had to be dealt with immediately and the power inherent in unified oblast committees restored. Otherwise, a split in the Party could occur, with clashes arising over competition for funds, seats in the Supreme Soviet, membership in the Central Committee, budget appropriations, and extend to all aspects of political life. Who could tell where all the dividing and subdividing would end? Even the splitting of the KGB into two sections was no longer inconceivable!

Perhaps the nucleus of a two-party system could have been a progressive and ultimately successful stage in the nation's development, but the Communist Party was not yet ready for such a transformation. Clearly duality of power in the oblasts could be eliminated only by the removal of Khrushchev himself. At the beginning of 1963 no one knew just when this might happen—it could take up to several years but, in any case, the regular Party Congress, due to convene either in late 1964 or early 1965, would decide his fate and return the Party to its accustomed state of unified territorial power. The kings wanted the return of their kingdoms, even it if meant sacrificing the emperor. Only some astonishing success—an agricultural miracle that endured—could save Khrushchev.

In 1963 he was celebrating a double anniversary of his reign—ten years as First Secretary and five years as Chairman of the Council of Ministers. He was warmly praised in the press, in speeches, and in films. There were multivolume editions of his writings, his portraits appeared in the press every day in one or another situation. Newsreels covered his activities with renewed fervor—everything seemed to indicate that this tenth anniversary celebration would indeed be triumphant. But most unfortunately for Khrushchev, it was agriculture, his own "territory," the area to which he had devoted so much of his energies, that was the source of even more calamitous developments in 1963.

chapter fourteen

THE
SOUR TASTE OF FAILURE

IN 1963 a drought struck some sections of the Soviet Union. It was not as severe as others had been in the past, nor did it extend over a vast area. Nevertheless, this moderate drought compounded a situation that threatened whole regions with famine. In 1953, after a similar crop failure, Khrushchev had denounced Malenkov for allowing strategic grain supplies from state reserves to be sold to the public; he passionately declared that strategic grain reserves must be preserved inviolate at all cost. Ten years later he was to find himself in an identical situation.

At first the 1963 drought did not arouse any general apprehension. Nearly eight years of official propaganda had convinced people that the nation's production of foodstuffs had almost doubled since 1953. Of course, there might be an occasional crop failure, but it was generally assumed that in eight or nine years' time the government would surely have accumulated sufficient stockpiles to ward off famine. However as early as September 1963, when the celebration of Khrushchev's tenth anniversary as First Secretary was to be observed, bread supplies in large areas of the south, the Ukraine, the northern Caucasus, and the Transcaucasus fell off sharply. People stood in long lines for hours to buy two or three kilos of bread. Soon stores had to limit what one person could buy. Flour disappeared completely from their shelves. Bread supplies remained satisfactory in Moscow and Leningrad, but people from nearby towns arrived in the capital by the thousands to buy food. It then became apparent that the government had no reserves of grain in its storehouses.

By all indications the 1963 harvest was not large enough to feed the nation until the 1964 harvest was available if unrestricted sales continued. To assure the nation's food supply, it might once again be necessary to introduce an official ration system, a system that had been dispensed with after the war.

The situation was acutely embarrassing for Khrushchev.

He realized that hunger in the southern regions would spread alarm throughout the Soviet Union and that the agricultural crisis that loomed on the horizon offered no possibility of easy resolution. Calamity could be averted only by enormous purchases of grain and other foodstuffs from abroad, although this would be the first time that such extensive emergency measures had ever been required, either in tsarist or Soviet history. But there were not enough hard currency reserves to pay for such a purchase, and Khrushchev was forced into a drastic decision—to use not only such hard currency reserves as were on hand but also to part with some of the country's gold stockpile. Ingots were shipped to the London gold market, the first consignment a total of 500 tons. Trade delegations purchased grain in many countries, mainly Canada, Australia, and even from West Germany and France. A small amount was bought in the United States. A consignment of rye was purchased in Finland. At the same time, the import of other foodstuffs had to be increased—meat from Australia and South

America, butter from New Zealand and the Scandinavian countries, poultry and various canned goods. Even canned meat was purchased from China. The Soviet Union, the largest agricultural country in the world, had fallen into agricultural dependency on capitalist countries, a dependency from which it has not yet been able to extricate itself.

FURTHER HARASSMENTS

The food disaster of 1963 was not brought on by the drought alone, but was the consequence of a number of interrelated factors that had caused increasing dislocation and disorder since 1959. When in 1959 it had become apparent that Soviet agriculture would not meet the highly inflated goals of the new "Seven-Year Plan," the blame was then (as is often the case) put on the kolkhozniks. A favorite accusation was that they did too little work on the kolkhoz itself and devoted too much time to their own household plots. In 1961 and 1962 Khrushchev revived the policy of penalizing farm workers, trying through economic pressures to make them concentrate their efforts on the kolkhoz work and be more dependent on its output. Tight controls were imposed—even the planting of potatoes was strictly limited.

In the press, a major campaign was unleashed against the private plots, which were declared to be a relic of capitalism. Kolkhozniks who sold their own produce in the free market were branded as "speculators." However, household plots accounted for a substantial portion of the country's total food output. According to economists, in the late 1950s some 80 percent of the produce grown on private plots was consumed within the peasant family and only 20 percent was sold outside; but this 20 percent comprised not less than 50 percent of the fresh vegetables and 30 percent of the fresh fruit available in the cities.

Under all the harassment and name-calling, foodstuff output in the private sector dropped sharply. In kolkhoz markets where free trade was allowed, the sale of foodstuffs markedly decreased between 1959 and 1962, and market prices rose. Thus the growing urban population became even more dependent on government food supplies, as did millions of peasant families whose drive and initiative had been thoroughly stifled.

In addition, newly increased quotas for meat forced many kolkhoz chairmen to demand that kolkhoznik's sell their private livestock to the collective farm. In 1959 alone, more than 3 million cows were "purchased" in this way. By January 1963, kolkhozniks owned only about 10 million cows instead of the 22 million that had belonged to them in 1958.* The number of privately owned pigs, sheep, goats, and fowl also decreased significantly.

But even worse, livestock that had been forcibly purchased from individuals and integrated into kolkhoz herds were not being adequately fed. In the Ukraine, for example, livestock purchases from the kolkhozniks increased the number of animals in kolkhoz herds by 43 percent, while the amount of feed allocated to them increased by only 1 percent.† As a result, aggregate meat and milk production did not reflect the increased size of collective herds—change was either nonexistent or for the worse. When 12 million cattle previously maintained by their owners were transferred to collective farm ownership, the farms needed much more fodder, and far from selling supplies to the state they in fact became dependent on the state as a source of feed grain. Furthermore, because individuals were no longer allowed to own livestock, they stopped planting feed

---

* *Narodnoe khoziaistvo SSSR v 1963g* (The National Economy of the Soviet Union in 1963) (Moscow: Central Statistical Administration [TsSU], 1964), pp. 313–14.

† *Voprosy ekonomiki* (Problems of Economics), 1965, No. 8, p. 25.

crops on their household plots. The kolkhozes should have increased their herds gradually, keeping pace with the growth of feed supplies and not by virtually confiscating their members' cows. Promises made to those who gave up livestock—that they would be supplied with milk, butter, and meat from kolkhoz stocks—were not kept, and hardly could be in the light of scarce supplies. The average yield of milk per cow decreased throughout the country because of fodder shortages, and even the cities were in need.

At the same time a restriction was placed on raising livestock in suburban areas, a practice that had previously been encouraged. Khrushchev, who in 1953 had avowed that people living in the suburbs or small towns could own their own livestock, now offered to the Supreme Soviet a proposal for a law that would forbid these people to keep livestock. This law was popularly dubbed the "cow law," * and was enacted primarily because, without enough feed for the "public" herds, the government was not in a position to sell feed to individuals as it had done earlier. Some suburban residents bought bread to feed their animals, and so purchase of bread for this purpose was declared a criminal act, punishable by imprisonment.

All these measures were grievously unpopular, particularly among the peasants, and were far from inspiring people to work harder and longer to increase output. In such a situation *overfulfillment* of grain and other agricultural quotas would be insufficient to provide the population with foodstuffs and to assure adequate feed for livestock. Hence any shortfalls in planned production because of bad weather conditions, even though minor, could only lead to disaster.

* In the Russian phrase *skotsky zakon*, the adjective *skotsky* literally means "pertaining to cattle" (in the broad sense of any domesticated herd animals), but it is derived from the noun *skot*, which when applied to humans is more or less equivalent to English pejorative senses of "swine" or "beasts." Thus the usage here is a rather apt pun. (Translator's note)

THE MISUSE OF FALLOW FIELDS

A second irrational scheme that compounded the damage wrought by drought was the cultivation of fields supposed to be fallow. For centuries Russian peasants knew that fields left fallow in the summer, but plowed in fall and spring and weeded regularly, accumulated moisture and nutritive substances and by the end of the following summer were ready for *early planting* of winter crops (e.g., winter wheat could be sown at the end of August). Only in our own century has science demonstrated that land left fallow in the summer builds up nitrogen (through the action of nitrogen-fixing microbes) and other nutritive substances and also holds moisture because of the favorable structure of the soil. Winter crops sown on such land in late summer or early autumn produce a large vegetative mass and a good deep root system in the autumn and thus face the winter with a well-protected root system. In spring reproductive growth rapidly occurs; harvest time comes early, before the arrival of droughts common in the latter half of summer. Such winter crops obviously have a great advantage over crops planted in the spring.

But Khrushchev and many of his advisers regarded a field lying fallow in the summer as nothing more than an *empty* field—it was simply a waste to leave it unplanted! He was particularly influenced by the views of G. A. Nalivaiko, director of the Altai Agricultural Institute, and by Roswell Garst, the American farmer from Iowa. Both were in fact relying on misleading data, valid only for intensive cultivation with adequate supplies of fertilizers as well as herbicides to combat weeds, but both fertilizers and herbicides were not yet available in great enough quantities to adopt this system.

The area of land normally fallow in the summer was approximately 18 million hectares. Khrushchev, as usual, could not wait to experiment on a small scale and, in 1962, launched a heavy campaign to eliminate two-thirds of it—nearly 11 to 12 million hectares were planted with crops, mainly corn and sunflowers. But Khrushchev's hopes were not realized. Although the area under cultivation was substantially increased, the 1962 harvest was only very slightly larger than that of 1961.

Moreover, because fields normally fallow were now unavailable for an early planting date, winter crops had to be sown a month to six weeks later than the ideal time and, even worse, be sown on weary soil where other crops had just been harvested. There was too little time for roots and vegetative mass to develop before the cold set in. The severe winter of 1963 destroyed these late-sown crops, whereas crops planted on fallow land (a few million hectares had been left alone) survived the winter well.

The drought of 1963 occurred somewhat late, in the second half of the summer. Winter crops that had been sown on fallow fields did not suffer, but spring crops planted to replace the lost late-sown winter ones suffered enormously.

Spring plantings in the virgin lands were also affected by the drought. Spring crops followed by a regular crop were totally killed, but winter crops planted on fallow land did not have a bad yield even in the virgin lands. The proportion was too insignificant, however, to make much difference in the overall picture.

Thus it was that two drastic mistakes of 1962—restrictions on private plots and abandonment of the practice of letting land lie fallow in the summer—transformed the minor drought of 1963 into a serious national agricultural disaster.

Khrushchev belatedly recognized his mistake. At the Central Committee Plenum in December 1963 he admitted, with numerous qualifications, the necessity of fallow land in summer in those areas of the Soviet Union subject to periodic drought. It was clear to all agriculturally oriented Party members attending the Plenum exactly why it had suddenly become necessary to purchase 12 million tons of foreign grain, an amount which could have been reaped within the borders of the Soviet Union had the land been allowed to be fallow in the customary way (20 to 25 million tons could have been grown with a little effort).

Khrushchev's decision to permit a return to the traditional crop cycle was greeted with stormy applause from all those present. This response was an expression of the basic hope that people would no longer have to stand in long lines in order to buy bread made of Canadian wheat, meat imported from Argentina, butter from Denmark, eggs from Poland, chickens from Bulgaria, and vegetables from Bulgaria and Rumania.

FERTILIZER IN THE FOREGROUND

After the 1963 drought, Khrushchev finally realized that the "virgin lands" program, originally intended as a temporary measure to gain time for the development of agriculture in the traditional farming regions, had actually held back any such development. The bitter lesson of 1963 forced him to look at the situation in a new way. But here too his unbridled "enthusiasm" blinded his vision.

When predictions for a bad harvest became a certainty, Khrushchev at last had to acknowledge that any spectacular flowering of agriculture would be heavily dependent on modern fertilizers. Characteristically, he set a staggering target for the Soviet chemical industry—to expand the production of fertilizers to 100 million tons by 1970 (i.e., a fivefold increase in seven years). To reach this grandiose objective, the yearly increase in fertilizer output would have to be 12 million tons—ten times greater than the annual increase from 1953 to 1963. (Again the Soviet Union was to "overtake the United States.")

Khrushchev announced his unrealistic program without consulting the appropriate planning bodies or agrochemical/ fertilizer experts and without considering the lessons of history. Production of the chemical fertilizers which helped the United States and Europe reach very high yields lagged very far behind in the Soviet Union. In 1937, only some 3 million tons were produced—far too little for such a vast country. Any one of the smaller countries of Western Europe was turning out more. After the war, fertilizer production increased although planned levels were never achieved. By 1950 only 5.5 million tons were produced—only a third of what had been intended. A 1953 drive to increase output to 17 million tons was not fulfilled as production leveled off at 13 million tons.* Out of all the goals laid down for agricultural development, the manufacture of fertilizers remained furthest from attainment, by a margin of 40 to 45 percent. Only in 1962 did fertilizer production reach the 17 million tons that had been the target as far back as 1950. But even in 1962, the Soviet Union used only a third as much chemical fertilizer per hectare as the United States, a seventh as much as France, an eleventh as much as England, and a fifteenth as much as West Germany. In addition, those fertilizers that were used were ungranulated and of poor quality. Weed-killers were hardly used at all.

Not only was there almost no storage space for fertilizers on the kolkhozes, there were no special railroad cars for shipping them. According to government data, almost one quarter of the fertilizer produced was therefore lost or spoiled before it reached the fields. Furthermore, the kolkhozes had no machinery to spread fertilizer so the work was often done laboriously by hand.

Thus Khrushchev's sudden leap to a goal of 100 million tons with an annual *increase* in output of 12 million tons (bearing in mind that over the preceding thirty years the highest *total* amount—not an increase—produced in one year had been 17 million tons) was quite absurd. When Khrushchev was firmly told the hard facts, he had to find justification for settling on a

* *Narodnoe khoziaistvo SSSR v 1962g* (The National Economy of the Soviet Union) (Moscow: Central Statistical Administration [TsSU], 1963), p. 165.

lower figure so that he could retreat without loss of face. First
he scheduled a special Plenum of the Central Committee. The
Committee then requested a group of prominent scientists,
chemists, and agrochemists to compose and then make public a
letter in which they were to suggest a moderation of the 100
million tons target figure and propose the allocation of more
funds to construct storage facilities and improve the quality of
fertilizers and methods of application. Thus, Khrushchev could
solemnly "take the scientists' suggestions into consideration"
and propose not 100 million tons, but 70 to 80 million, and an
annual growth rate of 7 to 9 million tons rather than 12 million.

But even these more modest figures could not be realized.
Not more than 50 to 60 percent of this target was met and a
large part of the fertilizer produced was not made available to
produce wheat and other grain cultures but was instead held
back for specialized crops (cotton, sunflowers, and others).

Thus the mild drought of 1963 (its harmful effects compounded by the foolish measures taken with regard to household plots and fallow lands), along with the failure of the fertilizer program to help the agricultural situation, was to make
1964 an even greater crisis year for Khrushchev than 1957 had
been.

THE REACTION TO KHRUSHCHEV'S REMEDY

Desperately Khrushchev held one Plenum of the Party Central Committee after another, all of them devoted to agricultural
questions. But no miraculous solutions presented themselves.

Upon returning from a trip to Denmark and Sweden, he presented still another new plan to the Presidium, this time one for
the radical transformation of the entire agricultural administrative system. It was scheduled to be put before the Plenum of the
Central Committee in November. In his plan Khrushchev proposed establishing twelve state committees in Moscow to direct

twelve individual specialized branches of agriculture: animal husbandry, poultry-raising, grain production, soil improvement, mechanization, the use of chemical fertilizers, etc. Each committee would have a staff of not less than 500 or 600 specialists in its given field. A draft of the proposal was sent not only to the Presidium of the Central Committee but to all oblast committees as well. By August frantic Party conferences were held across the land. It was obvious to everyone that, once again, a Khrushchev project was totally unworkable. It would mean not just dual (agricultural/industrial) authority, but a total fragmentation of management. Oblast committee secretaries were already unhappy over their divided status, but now those concerned with agriculture would have twelve different superiors in Moscow.

The reaction to Khrushchev's "Preliminary Report" strengthened the position of those Central Committee members and oblast secretaries who were against him. It was not a "conspiracy" like the one organized by Malenkov, Molotov, and Kaganovich in 1957. Many of those who were most deeply convinced that Khrushchev had to go would have welcomed grounds for believing otherwise. There was no clear-cut leader to replace him. Almost all the members of the Presidium and many members of the Plenum owed their present high status to Khrushchev. They all had at one time worked with him enthusiastically, and had supported and been part of his rise to power. But the unavoidable step had to be taken. Governing a vast country like the Soviet Union in the midst of a complex scientific and technological revolution was beyond the powers of any one man, and this was particularly the case when that man not only lacked all the expertise required but even more important, did not have the necessary patience or a common-sense ability to accept experienced advice.

Khrushchev's critics were the first to admit the goodness of his intentions but quoted the cliché about "the road to hell." Whatever Khrushchev's worthy personal qualities, he was leading the country and, most importantly (for oblast committee and Central Committee members) the Party, to disaster; he was undermining the bases of Party supremacy, of Party unity, and had threatened security of tenure in key Party posts. "We do not want or need any more reorganizations," argued his critics. "We must return to old reliable forms of secure and stable centralized leadership." With these ideas in mind, they were determined to remove Khrushchev from power.

chapter fifteen

EXIT KHRUSHCHEV

THE men determined to remove Khrushchev from the center of control did not want to repeat the mistakes made in 1957. Slowly and deliberately they worked out their strategy. Ultimately Khrushchev would be stripped of power at a plenary meeting of the Party Central Committee, but first it was necessary to hold a preparatory meeting of the Presidium to discuss and to approve the main report citing the mistakes, the arbitrary actions, and the autocratic, personal character of Khrushchev's methods, which violated the principle of collective leadership, one of the cornerstones of Party Law. A circumstance that made these preparatory discussions somewhat easier was the fact that Khrushchev was enjoying an October vacation at his dacha on Cape Pitsunda on the Black Sea not far from Sochi. This was also the location of an extraordinary botanical phenomenon, the only surviving forest of ancient pines; an ugly concrete wall several miles long stretched around two-thirds of the cape, behind which stood Khrushchev's villa, not far from the sea. It was here that he spent the last days of his political career.

When the plans for Khrushchev's ouster were formulated in October 1964, his popularity was at low ebb among virtually all components of the population from Party leaders down to kol-khozniks. At this time there was not a single power group of any size—whether scientists, doctors, writers, educators, artists, business or industrial executives, factory or office workers, military officers, young people or old—that would have been willing to offer Khrushchev its backing and support. Nor were there any factions within the Party or government hierarchy who were pro-Khrushchev, with the exception of a small coterie of personal aides who, although occupying important positions, lacked any real individual power. Thus Khrushchev's ouster could be carried out through regular legal procedures (a meeting of the Presidium of the Central Committee and a plenum) and there was no need for a "conspiracy" as in 1957.

At that time, the key figures (Molotov, Malenkov, and Kaganovich) had sought to keep the general membership of the Central Committee unaware of what they were planning. In 1964 the procedure was quite different; before the final resolution was to be formally presented to the officially convened Plenum, members of the Central Committee were summoned from their oblasts in early October and informed either individually or in small groups of the plan to oust Khrushchev. These discussion groups were briefed mainly by Suslov. Of the more than 200 members of the full Central Committee only three did not accept the projected decision—the Central Committee Secretary for Agriculture, V. J. Poliakov, the Secretary of the Leningrad oblast committee, V. S. Tolstikov, and one member of the Secretariat of the Party Central Committee of the Ukraine. According to some accounts, the Ukrainian representative tried to call Khrushchev and warn him, but was unable to get through. Evidently, the telephone system at Khrushchev's Black Sea residence was already under surveillance.

The Presidium of the Central Committee convened on October 11, 1964, to deliberate the question of Khrushchev's removal. Mikoyan was not present, as he too was vacationing, not far from Khrushchev. (Contrary to the current version of these events, Mikoyan, who was a close friend of Khrushchev's, was not informed of what was being planned.) Frol Kozlov, one of those who had saved Khrushchev in 1957, was seriously ill and also did not participate. Besides the members and candidate members of the Presidium, A. A. Gromyko, Minister of Foreign Affairs, and a number of oblast committee secretaries attended (twenty-two persons in all). Although R. Malinovsky, the Minister of Defense, V. Semitchastny, Chairman of the KGB, and other army, state security, and police officials were fully au courant and supported the resolution being prepared, nevertheless special security measures were taken to isolate Khrushchev from the time the first preparations for the meeting began until the final resolution was actually adopted.

In the foreign press, the "unexpectedness" of Khrushchev's downfall gave rise to sensational rumors of a "plot" or a "coup." Actually, the organizers took elaborate care to keep all measures within the limits of constitutional and Party procedure and to avoid any possible cause for unrest in the country at large. Originally, it had been intended that Khrushchev retain his membership in the Central Committee, since the election or removal of members of the Central Committee is the prerogative of the Party Congress. However, Khrushchev's initial furious reaction and rude and insulting behavior later at the Presidium meeting made this impossible. The principal address at the Plenum meeting would be delivered by Suslov, although it was decided that Brezhnev would be elected First Secretary.

By this time, the Kremlin was absolutely incommunicado and, of course, all of Khrushchev's lines of communication were tightly controlled. On October 11, a call was put through to Khrushchev to inform him that a Presidium meeting was taking place. The reason for the meeting (which Khrushchev had not expected), according to Brezhnev, who conducted the conversation, was to discuss Khrushchev's plan for the further splintering of agricultural organization, his "Preliminary Report," described earlier.

Khrushchev at first declined (and rather rudely at that) to come on such short notice. (Mikoyan, also called to Moscow, had already gone.) After a short interval, Brezhnev informed Khrushchev that in the event of his refusal to fly to Moscow, the Presidium would begin its deliberations without him. After that, Khrushchev agreed to leave for Moscow at once. A military plane, rather than his private plane, was provided. Upon landing in Moscow, Khrushchev gave directions that he be taken to his home, but his escort refused to obey, and he was informed that there was a prior order that he appear at the Kremlin immediately.

The Presidium meeting lasted until late at night on October 13. Only Mikoyan for a time stood against Khrushchev's removal, but subsequently he joined the majority. Khrushchev at first would not agree to retire voluntarily and demanded that a full Plenum of the Central Committee be convened. He was hoping that, as in 1957, he would manage to gain the support of a Plenum majority. But during a break in the meeting on the night of October 13, Mikoyan persuaded Khrushchev that he would be wise to submit voluntarily a statement requesting retirement. The wording of the resignation, later published in the press, was also worked out at this time. Because of his "cooperation," it was decided that, at the Plenum of the Central Committee scheduled for the afternoon of October 14, there would be no extensive debate and no bitter public denunciation of Khrushchev.

The Presidium continued its session in the morning of October 14, and in the afternoon the very well briefed full membership of the Plenum was convened. The Plenum was opened by Brezhnev, with Mikoyan presiding. Suslov reported on

Khrushchev's removal and the basic reasons for the decision. He directed many hostile comments at the embattled leader. The proposal to relieve Khrushchev of his duties as First Secretary and Chairman of the Council of Ministers and to drop him from membership in the Central Committee was passed *unanimously* and without debate.

Suslov's report dwelt on Khrushchev's misguided agricultural and economic policy. In addition, he was accused of attempting to create a "Khrushchev cult," of having abused power, of having a small unofficial "cabinet" of friends and relatives as advisers instead of consulting the Presidium, and of bringing his entire family into politics—his son-in-law, A. Adzhubei, the editor of *Izvestia*, functioned as a sort of unofficial "minister of foreign affairs" and many foreign policy decisions had been made without consulting Gromyko, a rather confusing state of affairs for Soviet ambassadors abroad. Among Khrushchev's various foreign policy decisions under attack were the awarding of the title of Hero of the Soviet Union to President Nasser and Vice-President Amer of the United Arab Republic, and the construction of a large and costly stadium in Indonesia when the people in that country were acutely in need of food.

After Khrushchev's ouster, Adzhubei, P. Satiukov, editor of *Pravda,* and Kharlamov, Chairman of the State Committee on Radio and Television, all were dismissed for having fostered a "Khrushchev cult," as was V. Poliakov, the Central Committee's Secretary of Agriculture. No other major reshuffling took place within the Party or the government. There was a resolution that the posts of First Secretary of the Central Committee and Chairman of the Council of Ministers be forever separate (Kosygin was recommended for the latter office).

In the West, the story of Khrushchev's ouster has been widely discussed and written about and the general sequence of events is well known. In the Soviet press, no details whatever were published; however, after October 16 members of the Presidium and other senior officials of the Central Committee traveled throughout the country to meet Party activists and explain the decisions that had been made and the reasons behind them. As a result of these "closed" meetings, a good deal of what had taken place in Moscow from October 12 to October 15 gradually leaked out.

Suslov had been chosen to give the major speech because he was not under obligation to Khrushchev for his successful career but had already been a Presidium member under Stalin, while most of the other members owed their advancement to Khrushchev. They had all wanted to ride his bandwagon in its heyday and this was to have an interesting effect on what happened after it broke down. Although under Khrushchev there had been no collective leadership, there had been collective responsibility. Thus after Khrushchev's dismissal, there was no open discussion or official condemnation of his policies as the Central Committee and its Presidium had played an active role implementing the various projects and reorganizations now under fire. For this reason, neither Suslov's speech nor the minutes of the meeting were ever published, and at the subsequent briefings for Party activists only a few of the accusations against Khrushchev were discussed. Brezhnev, after his election as First Secretary of the Central Committee, declared: "We should not pour muck on ourselves"; he recommended that as far as non-Party persons and the press were concerned, there should be no elaboration of the reasons for Khrushchev's removal beyond what was contained in the official version released to the newspapers (i.e., that Khrushchev had been relieved of his responsibilities at his own request because of age and ill health).

The "resignation" of Khrushchev and other changes in Kremlin leadership were greeted apathetically by the general populace. It is said that Brezhnev was astonished when the head of the KGB informed him that no public demonstrations or even a single statement had been reported anywhere in the country in support of Khrushchev. After all, for more than ten years his activities had been constantly acclaimed in all the media and his photograph had appeared virtually every day. Also, many of his programs had, indeed, benefited a great number of people.

Little is known about Khrushchev's life in retirement. After his ouster, he was treated with rather more circumspection than he had shown toward Malenkov or Bulganin. He was granted a generous pension, and was allowed to retain his Moscow apartment and villa just outside the city.* A car and chauffeur were put at his disposal, as well as a small staff to guard his country home—and apparently to keep him under surveillance as well. Sometimes he was even allowed to meet with foreign correspondents, but their interviews were not mentioned in the Soviet press.

In the first months after his retirement Khrushchev was almost continually in a state of depression and seldom left the grounds of his dacha. But by 1966, reconciled to life as a pensioner, he began to visit Moscow, attend the theater or cinema, or meet informally with artists and writers he knew and admired. Sometimes he would simply stroll about the streets of Moscow; people of course recognized him and sometimes began a conversation. While on these walks he would be accompanied by security agents who did not, however, interfere with his activities, but let him chat with whom he wished. Sometimes he would ask old friends to his country home, but the majority of those invited would usually decline on some pretext or other. He liked to listen to foreign radio broadcasts in Russian, especially those of the BBC.

---

* During his years in power, Khrushchev, like most members of the Party Presidium and top-level government figures, enjoyed four residences: an apartment in Moscow, a luxurious townhouse in Moscow with all services provided by the state, a country home just outside the city, and a summer dacha on the Black Sea. The Moscow apartment and country home are considered a leader's own property and can be left to his family in case of his death; the Moscow townhouse and the Black Sea dacha revert to the government after he leaves office.

During walks around the country community where he lived, Khrushchev enjoyed complete freedom. He would sometimes wander quite far, looking over the fields of the nearby farms. Once during such an excursion he noticed a very poorly cultivated field and asked a field worker to fetch the foreman and the director. Then and there he began to reprove them severely, (with justification) for improper cultivation and slipshod work. By force of habit he did not merely voice his opinions but specified corrections and issued commands. At first the officials were courteous although confused but finally the director, stung by the sharpness of Khrushchev's rather apt comments, took affront and replied in no less blunt a tone: "You're not the Chairman of the Council of Ministers any more and you don't have the right to meddle in our farm's affairs—we know what we're supposed to do ourselves." For a long time afterwards, this incident rankled in Khrushchev's memory.

Seven long years of relative obscurity dragged by. Then on September 13, 1971, the world learned that Khrushchev had died two days previously in a Moscow hospital following a heart attack. TASS, the Soviet press agency, carried a terse item in which the Central Committee and the government expressed "sorrow" at the death of "honorary pensioner Khrushchev."

The burial service did not take place in the small cemetery just outside the Kremlin wall near the Lenin Mausoleum, the usual site for top Party and state leaders or for virtual heroes (like cosmonaut Yuri Gagarin) but in the cemetery of the former Novodevichi monastery,* reserved for a lesser elite (academicians, deputy ministers, notable writers and artists, etc.).

---

* Novodevichi monastery with its cemetery is a major tourist attraction because of its famous monuments and sculpture. Here Khrushchev scored a final point. His monument, by Soviet sculptor Ernst Neizvestny, is an acknowledged work of art by a renowned artist. It is so impressive that more than a year went by before the necessary permission to install it was granted. In the small cemetery near the Kremlin, large monuments are not permitted and the graves are rather modest.

Ordinary people cannot be buried in Novodevichi; permission from the Moscow Council is necessary. (For burial in the small cemetery near the Kremlin, however, permission from the Party Presidium is required.) The simple ceremony was witnessed by about 150 persons, including Khrushchev's immediate family and several former political prisoners who owed their return to civilian life to him. No Soviet official attended although the Party Central Committee sent an impressive wreath.

chapter sixteen

AFTER KHRUSHCHEV

KHRUSHCHEV'S departure from the political arena did not create a vacuum as was the case after Stalin's death, and there was no question of a prolonged political struggle. A truly *collective* leadership emerged, which was also more conservative in character. It was composed of many of the faces that are still with us (1976)—Leonid Brezhnev as First Secretary (a position later changed to Secretary General to increase its authority), Alexei Kosygin as Premier, and Nikolai Podgorny as Chairman of the Presidium.

As might have been expected, a reexamination and reversal of almost all of Khrushchev's domestic innovations and foreign policies was soon under way. The former by-territory system of organization for oblast Party committees was restored and consolidated raions were broken up. The division of the Party and governmental hierarchy into agricultural and industrial sectors was abolished from top to bottom. The Economic Councils (*sovnarchozy*) were done away with at all levels, as were most state committees, and the more traditional ministries were reestablished and given even broader powers for directing their particular branches of industry. The Ministry of Agriculture for the Soviet Union and the Ministry of Agriculture for the Russian SSR returned from their rural exile to Moscow, occupying the same comfortable quarters they had enjoyed before "going out to the land." Agricultural ministries of all the individual national republics also moved back to their respective capital cities. The plan to set up agricultural education centers in special "agrotowns" was permanently shelved and, once more, the Timiriazev Agricultural Academy in Moscow was allowed to open its doors to first-year students. Lysenko was stripped of his policy-making powers and the teaching of genetics and genetic research was brought into line with modern science. A plenum on agriculture was postponed until 1965 to allow time to work out means of undoing the consequences of Khrushchev's innovations. Among measures contemplated were reducing the virgin lands area, restoring kolkhozniks' household plots to their former size, and ending restrictions on private ownership of livestock. There was talk of economic reform in industry, of modifying the rigid standardization of housing and industrial construction, and of many other economic changes.

Religious persecution and harassment abated and the Orthodox Church was allowed to conduct services and to circulate ecclesiastical literature—within Church circles. Restoration began on many churches and monasteries of cultural or historical importance. The Kremlin realized that the Church, now under strict state control, would be an ally; rather than condone opposition, it would promote conformity. Religious observance in Russia had always been strongest in the villages; therefore the reopening of village churches and the revival of services in rural areas halted the drift to the cities—an added bonus.

Khrushchev's "reform" of secondary education was dropped; the eleven-year polytechnic program was replaced by the traditional ten-year program of general education, although special technical and professional schools were opened for fourteen- or fifteen-year-olds preferring to be trained in a particular trade.

The economical but unimaginative specifications for apartment-house construction, typical of the Khrushchev period, as well as the dull and uniform designs for administrative buildings were put aside. In Moscow and in other cities construction of individually designed buildings flourished. Even existing standardized projects were made more attractive if possible. Today in any city in the Soviet Union one can easily distinguish those districts built in Stalin's day (housing for the ruling elite), the extensive, unattractive, but rapidly constructed housing of the Khrushchev period (the *khrushchoby* or "Khrushchev slums"), and residential districts of more contemporary architectural style.

None of these changes occurred overnight and their impact could be felt only in the course of several years. This was especially true for agriculture.

In the spring of 1965, when the farmer was given freedom of choice, corn acreage sharply decreased. The day of clover and other perennial grasses returned. Countryside discontent was mollified, although many of Khrushchev's policies left an indelible mark. It was impossible to re-open the defunct machine-tractor stations, nor could all those who had left the villages be magically returned. Over such a vast territory economic change took place very slowly and the basic causes of agricultural decline were still present for many years after Khrushchev's eclipse.

The hated innovation in Party rules requiring mandatory replacement of one-third of Central Committee and oblast committee members at every election was quickly rescinded and those high-level officials who had lost their important posts were returned to the circles of the elite, although at a lower level (they were made deputy ministers, ministers of Union Republics, secretaries of oblast committees, chairmen of oblast executive committees, or were sent abroad as ambassadors). All these changes were made gradually without the element of erratic surprise characteristic of the Khrushchev period.

The chief international problem inherited from Khrushchev, the conflict with China, was not resolved. The Chinese press greeted Khrushchev's removal with delight, but its criticisms focused on his foreign policy, which certainly had to be continued by the new regime.

It was inevitable that the ouster of Khrushchev, an initiator of liberal political reforms, led to a resurgence of conservative trends, to the appearance of so-called "neo-Stalinist" tendencies. As Khrushchev's name vanished from the pages of the daily press, references to Stalin began to reappear in a favorable context. The Army was built up once again to counteract the unilateral troop reductions and cut-backs in military budget undertaken by Khrushchev. The KGB apparatus, in Khrushchev's day almost entirely drained of strength, once again acquired considerable muscle. Khrushchev had considered himself a leader whose power was vested above all in his own popularity and personal prestige. Since the new leadership could not as yet rely on the popularity of any one or any combination of its members, its aim was to strengthen the power of the Party and the State apparatus—thus the KGB was given much greater authority. The political presence of the Army also made itself felt and its influence, typical of the military, was conservative and authoritarian in nature.

Once at leisure, Khrushchev was compelled to reflect on his failure, on what went wrong—particularly in agriculture—and apparently this is what inspired him to compile his memoirs. Ironically the memoirs reveal that even at the end Khrushchev could not grasp the fact that his misfortunes had not been due merely to the shortages of tractors, fertilizer, or good managers and dedicated farmers. Nor could his setbacks be blamed on the fact that the peasants did not know how to raise corn. The essence of the problem was that ever since the days of forced collectivization, people with a farmer's cast of mind, the true traditional peasants, had been virtually annihilated, overwhelmed by the ruthless attempt to make rural labor a variant of the industrial model, to transform the peasant-farmer into an industrial worker while denying him basic rights. A worker on a farm was bound to the land and subjected to bureaucratic discipline, a victim of governmental and bureaucratic insensitivity. If he had been allowed to labor freely as an independent farmer or as a member of a true cooperative with a tangible economic interest in his work, the story would have been very different indeed. It was in agriculture above all that individual initiative and personal freedom should have been encouraged.

And not only agriculture, but the entire economic development of the Soviet Union could have been more efficient and successful if, along with collectivization, the abolition of the entire private sector had not cut short the evolution of the highly productive individual workman. The story would also have been different if politically, instead of intensified authoritarian methods, there had been a gradual restoration of socialist democracy, even if only within the Party to begin with, and then gradually in the country at large.

Attempts by the new regime to achieve greater economic efficiency in the absence of major democratic political reforms were not successful. Its conservative tendencies culminated in military intervention in Czechoslovakia in 1968. However the Czechoslovak tragedy not only shocked the world but also lowered the prestige of the Soviet leaders to such a disastrous extent that they began to search for ways to regain popular appeal by means of internal reforms and a reexamination of foreign policy.

After a number of reforms in 1965 and the unraveling of Khrushchev's various reorganizations, overall economic development noticeably improved. In the ten years from 1964 to 1974 the Soviet Union made great strides in industrial development and the general standard of living rose substantially. However, even in this period it was agriculture that continued to lag far behind; crises were deferred but not averted. Expansion of industry was based on an increase in agricultural products, but the countryside was still too exhausted to assure such growth. The main problems continued to be the shortage of skilled persons capable of running agricultural machinery efficiently, the unwillingness of young people to work on the farms, the shortage of fertilizer because of the primitive state of the chemical industry, inequalities between urban and rural residents (no internal passports existed for rural residents,* which made it tedious if not impossible to change one's place of work or residence). Khrushchev had attempted, although unsuccessfully, to eliminate the need for the annual mobilization of urban factory and office workers, students, and grammar school pupils, to gather crops in late summer and fall. In 1965–72 city dwellers were dispatched to the countryside not only at that time but also to plant crops in the spring and gather hay in midsummer, while the autumn harvest became even more dependent on urban residents and the Army. The shortage of foodstuffs, inevitable under these circumstances, and the impossibility of amassing sizable state grain reserves led to agricultural crises in 1972 and 1975 even graver than the one in 1963. In 1972 Soviet purchases of foreign grain set world records (about 30 million tons, mostly from the United States), and disrupted the worldwide balance of food supplies. As a result, prices for grain and agricultural products rose everywhere, even in the United States, as did prices for cattle feed and meat.

This was indeed a paradoxical turn of events. The Soviet

---

* A new passport system, equal for urban and rural populations alike, was introduced in 1976 to help people migrate freely from the cities and towns to the countryside *and to return*. Before the new provision, a city person hesitated to move to a village to work because too often it turned out to be a one-way street—it was too difficult to get back again.

Union has the largest area of arable land of any country in the world as well as satisfactory (comparable with Canada) opportunities to develop agriculture and to export agricultural products. In this respect the Soviet Union must bear major responsibility for the world food situation. By purchasing grain and other agricultural products in enormous quantities, it forces up world prices for grain and other food products and thus decreases the availability of sustenance for poor nations suffering from periodic droughts and climatic disasters. In essence, two basic factors, the sharp rise in oil prices and the increase in food prices in 1973, have led to agricultural crisis and famine in a number of African and Asian countries. If in 1974 those countries which traditionally export grain and agricultural products had had surpluses similar to those in 1971, the consequences of the droughts and crop failures in the poorer countries would have been far less tragic.

The pressure of world food-supply problems has led to the adoption of a number of new agricultural reforms in the Soviet Union, the effect of which should become apparent in the not too distant future and which, it seems to us, should make the Soviet Union not an importer but an exporter of agricultural products.

One may reproach Khrushchev for much that he did, but there is also much for which he deserves credit. The historical consequences of Khrushchev's reforms have been quite contradictory. In agriculture and the economy his influence, in the later years of his rule, was most unfavorable—the adverse effects continue to be felt long after his departure, and have helped to create an international agricultural crisis. Although Khrushchev was responsible for sending arms to a number of Arab countries, and to some extent promoted the international conflicts that later erupted in this region, his impact on international affairs was not exclusively negative. It was Khrushchev who inaugurated the policy of mutual cooperation between the

Soviet Union, the United States, and Europe that has now become the "détente" of the 1970s. This policy was almost permanently shattered by a series of disparate yet related events: the
1968 invasion of Czechoslovakia, an intensification of the arms
race, U.S. escalation of the war in Vietnam, increasing Kremlin
intolerance toward democratic attitudes within the Soviet intelligentsia, and a further deterioration of relations between the
Soviet Union and China.

And yet the seeds of "live-and-let-live" planted by Khrushchev
have managed to survive—there continue to be signs of greater
tolerance between countries with different social systems. The
struggle he began for democratic transformations within the Soviet Union has not come to an end. It was Khrushchev who
declared that the superiority of one system or another should be
demonstrated not by military triumphs but by peaceful achievements. This was a fruitful sentiment appropriate for the postwar
years of the cold war.

The idea of peaceful competition at one time meant only a
rather expensive form of technical performance: the Soviet
Union launched the first man-made earth satellite and sent the
first man into space; the United States took up the challenge
and sent several three-man teams to the moon, thereby demon-
strating that American technology was still superior to Russian.
But the events of the last few years have shown that after all the
world has little need of these "cosmic" proofs of the superiority
of this or that political system.

Not so much conscious policy as the scientific-technological
revolution has made the world one, despite the problems of
race, religion, nationality, and ideology that remain as a legacy
from history. Khrushchev's contradictory activity in the Soviet
Union (which weakened the nation's economic potential), the
destructive tendencies of the Cultural Revolution in China, the
failure of Presidents Johnson and Nixon to win a military victory
in Vietnam and Cambodia, the stand-off resulting from the brief

though fierce war between Israel and the Arab countries, as well as the increasing hunger and want in the Third World countries (to whom both the United States and the Soviet Union want to prove the superiority of their respective social systems), all this has led to the realization that *competition* cannot be the guiding idea in structuring the future. What is needed is amity and cooperation between differing systems and above all cooperation among the most powerful "superpowers," the United States, the Soviet Union, and China. Only then will the smaller countries, which are more inclined to nationalistic and self-centered policies, become more restrained in the use of military means to achieve their goals.

The story of Khrushchev and his years in power shows quite clearly that in our modern, highly complex world, one single individual leader must not command excessive power within his own country nor exercise overwhelming influence on international events. The world must be freed from the danger of subjective decisions made by one or two human beings. No individual leader can deal with all the weighty problems of the modern world, even within a single fairly large country; those days are gone forever. We are now in an era of collective decisions, based on the interests of the whole world, of all humanity. "Great" political heroes were necessary in the era of empires, wars, and revolutions. But what the contemporary world needs most of all is well-educated, restrained, and sensible leaders, able to talk to one another and arrive at reasonable compromises. An excessive concentration of power in the hands of one individual, whether he is elected "President" by the general population, named "General Secretary" by a narrower group, or becomes head of state in some other way, is inappropriate for the extremely complex structure of modern society in these days of technological and economic interdependence. World problems can now be solved only by means of carefully thought-out scientific measures. The existence of differing socioeconomic systems in the world can be a source of friction, but alternatively it can be a foundation for amicable and mutually beneficial cooperation, as varying systems have diverse economic and technological capabilities, individual experiences, different potentials, their own particular advantages and drawbacks. Khrushchev made many mistakes whenever he tried to base his decisions on purely ideological foundations. He committed many errors because of an inadequate background and the narrowness of his views. And certainly his impatience often spoiled his attempts to reach otherwise attainable goals. But he was on much more solid ground and played a positive role in the history of the Soviet Union and of the entire world when he based his decisions on simple common sense and humane considerations. These principles clearly must prevail in the competent leadership which we anticipate from leaders in the future.